POLITICS OF REGION AND RELIGION IN INDIA

Politics of Region and Religion in India

Prabhat K. Datta
Reader in Political Science
University of Calcutta
Calcutta-700 051

UPPAL PUBLISHING HOUSE
New Delhi-110002

UPPAL PUBLISHING HOUSE
3, Ansari Road, Darya Ganj, New Delhi-110002

First Edition 1991
ISBN 81-85024-83-9

Printed in India
Published by B.S. Uppal for Uppal Publishing House, New Delhi-110002 and printed at Parashar Printers, New Seelampur, Delhi-110053

Dedicated
to

KALPANA AND SANJIB

PREFACE

The present volume is a collection of five essays which deal which some of the burning issues of Indian politics today. The first essay on the 'Rise of Regions in Indian Politics' originally grew out of my discussions in the class room. Besides identifying the roots of regionalism in India, it decries the tendency to brand all forms of regionalism as detrimental to the health of the country. The second essay entitled, 'Political Environment of India's Federalism', was prepared for presentation at the panel discussion on Centre-State Administrative Relations organised under the auspices of the annual conference of the Indian Public Administration Association held at Jodhpur in December, 1989. Its focus is on the political dimension of India's federalism. The third paper in this volume 'Secularism in India : A False Promise', was submitted at the international seminar on 'Emerging Contours of Socialism, Secularism and Democracy in India' organised by A.N. Sinha Centre of the P.G. Department of Public Administration at Patna in April, 1989. It attempts to expose the myth of secularism in India. The fourth paper on 'Reservation policy in India : Issues and Perspectives' was written for the seminar on Protective Discrimination in India organised by the J.N. Centre for Policy Research, Rewa (Madhya Pradesh) in July, 1990. The last paper in the volume 'From Ethnicity to Regionalism : The

Jharkhand Agitation' was written in 1987 when the third phase of the movement was gathering momentum.

For intellectual stimulation in course of writing these papers, I am indebted to Professor Mohit Bhattacharya, Vice-Chancellor, Burdwan University (West Bengal).

My wife and son have borne the burden of loneliness, while I had been busy writing these pieces. Hence, the book is dedicated to them.

Calcutta **Prabhat K. Datta**

CONTENTS

CHAPTER 1

Introduction

Contemporary Indian politics has been, analytically speaking, almost a baffling thing to the serious scholars and keen observers. To some, it is a resultant of the pursuit of Lakshmi, to others, it is a trayma of an old society being regulated by a new state, to some others who would requisition the whole repertoire of the Marxist concepts and categories in grappling with the meaning of Indian politics, the capitalist state is in deep crisis, and is gradually losing its legitimacy. There are still others to whom the pluralist conceptualization of society offers key to the understanding of Indian politics. Thus there is a variety of approaches which is indicative of intellectual groping for a proper conceptual framework for understanding politics in contemporary India. In this small book an attempt has been made to follow these lines of enquiry to analyse an extremely complex phenomenon called Contemporary Indian politics in a dynamic situation where forces of change are caused by factors within and without. An analyst has, therefore, to tread carefully and to a great extent, tentatively. This book seeks to examine some of the major issues, namely, regionalism, centre-state-relations, secularism and reservations. India is a country of continental proportion. There are many languages, many religions, many cultures and many traditions. It is essentially a multinational country. The British colonial rulers sought to develop a politically unified India as it suited imperial interests. They manipulated the inherent divisions in Indian society to consolidate their rule.

The nationalist movement provided a conducive atmosphere for the growth of national consciousness, as the one common enemy was the British colonial rulers. But Indian nationalism ever since its birth had assumed twin character—pan. Indian and regional. At the all India level the struggle against the British imperialism broke down the barriers of caste, language, religion etc. At the regional level dawned consciousness of the different nationalities. In the Independence struggle led by the Congress the two streams were combined by the national movement under the leadership of Gandhiji. The unified Indian national state emerged out of an all India movement.

After Independence power was transferred to the Indian National Congress. Indian state was captured by the bourgeoisie in alliance with the landlords in which the big bourgeoisie gave the leadership. Given the existence of the elements of the different modes of production in India there is a corresponding multiplicity of the ruling classes. In such a situation the ruling classes are compelled to function as an alliance even if the interests of the partners do not always converge at specific points of time. But the ruling classes have to forge a compromise. Historically an alliance of ruling classes can function effectively only under the leadership of a certain class. In India, the general consensus among the marxist scholars and activists has been to assign this role to the bourgeoisie. There are, however, serious differences of opinion among them about the nature of the Indian bourgeoisie.

Broadly speaking, the nature of Indian bourgeoisie is quite different from what Marx and Engels had observed about the western bourgeoisie. First, there was no imperialist or neo-imperialist bourgeoisie to lord over it. Secondly, in Europe the bourgeoisie of each nation state had to compete with its counterpart in other countries of Europe for the control of colonies. But the Indian bourgeoisie has no such opportunity of colonizing people. Capitalism in the west developed out of the massive exploitation of the colonial countries. Thirdly, the bourgeoisie in each of the western countries had to compete with bourgeoisie of approximately its own size and strength. But the Indian bourgeoisie has to compete with a bourgeoisie which is far bigger and stronger than it. Fourthly, the bourgeoisie in the west took 100 to 150 years to develop capitalism ; but its Indian counterpart (or for that matter, the bourgeoisie in other third world countries) has to have more rapid development of capitalism.

India adopted bourgeoisie democracy which thrived on the basis of a distinctive political culture. Bourgeois democratic structure was installed without the society having undergone the process of thorough capitalist transformation. The colonial rule denied Indian capitalism its natural right to go by the independent laws of growth. Bettleheim refers to little industrialization, low agricultural output, a low figure of national income per capita, very sluggish economic progress, considerable unemployment and under employment. These are some of the main characteristics of India's social and economic situation just after Independence.[1] Indian capitalism could not develop properly even after Independence as a result of the colonial hangover, renewed manoeuvres of world imperialism, dominance of monopoly capital etc. Bourgeois liberal democratic institutions were set in motion in a country where a fairly large majority of people are illiterate, ignorant, poverty sticken and steeped in traditional values and in a country the social fabric of which is characterized by the hierarchically structured caste system. Democracy began its journey in a thoroughly under-democratic environment. The social base was inappropriate and weak.

Bourgeois democratic institutions seemed to have been working well in the early years. Pt. Nehru was fond of bourgeois democratic virtues. He was a charismatic leader as Gandhiji was. He began casting the spell of his charisma throughout the country in matters relating to both party and government. There was none to challenge him. There was no voice of dissent. He sought to privatize if one can use the word Indian politics and administration, and seemed confident that he was capable of delivering goods to the people. The Congress won between 70 and 75 per cent seats in Parliament in the first three elections and between 61 and 68 per cent of the seats in the legislature although the percentage of electoral vote varied from 43 to 48 per cent.

Notwithstanding the constitutional promises and the unification of the country through the integration of provinces, problems of unity and democracy began to surface after the lapse of a few years as the first flush of the national victory faded. The social contradictions of Indian society which were underplayed during the freedom struggle now asserted themselves. The capatalist path of development revealed its own contradictions. Pt. Nehru had to yield to the pressures from below to reorganize India on the basis of language. This resulted in a shift in country's political life from an all-India to regional orientation.

Politics in India underwent a significant change in 1967 when the Indian National Congress lost its hegemony over the political scene in the country. It lost power in eight states. The ground was being prepared for the electoral and the organizational crises. The 'green revolution' in the 60s led to the rise of the regional bourgeoisie. The regional polititical parties and formations which came to prominance in 1967 represented the interests of the locally placed ruling class groups like the landlords and the kulaks in Punjab, or the Haryana, western UP etc., or the non-big bourgeoisie in Tamil Nadu. Javeed Alam says that the differentiation in landed interests between different states is due to differential distribution of investments and concessions by the Centre on top of the historically inherited consequences of land tenures, land development, productivity of land, crop specialization etc. In situations of economic crisis the inability of the state to dole out concessions to the dominant landed interests uniformly all over leads to discrimiation and consequent dissatisfactions. This is likely to lead to conflicts of interests within the same ruling class across the regions.[2] However, the 1967 elections were marked by the shift of the centre of gravity in Indian politics from the Centre to the region. This was a reaction to what has been called centrist politics in India.

The Congress Party suffered a split in ,969 following which Mrs. Gandhi rose to power. Mrs. Gandhi was an advocate of powerful state apparatus. She was confident of securing support of the big bourgeoisie and the rich peasants. The big bourgeoisie and the rich farmers were eager to have a strong and powerful Central Government. In 1969 the President of the FICCI (Federation of Indian Chambers of Commerce and Industry) moving the 'Resolution of National Integration and Business Community remarked that the Indian state made two most serious constitutional and administrative blunderes, namely, adoption of a federal constitution and reorganizing the federating units into linguistic states.[3] He said that the rise of the linguistic states was the cause of provincialism in its most ugly form. They found the democratic verdict of 1967-69 especially the victory of C.P.I. (M) in 1969 mid-term poll, 'as an alarming trend representing a dangerous turn toward regionalism'.[4]

Mrs. Gandhi's new coalition faced challenges from the state bosses who came from regional and sub-regional backgrounds. They had used caste, community and other parochial loyalties to build up their local power bases. They were opposed to the powerful champions of the national political culture which was developing in the wake of the new forces unleashed by the national planning, a growing national economy and modern communication system. Mrs. Gandhi's new coalition adopted a radical stance on domestic issues and anti-bossism in organisational matters. It was believed that this strategy would act as a double-edged sword. It would weaken the older leadership in the party, and would have the wider effect of securing eventually an extensive electoral mobilization across the traditional loyalties based on caste, community and other local considerations. All these paid dividents. Mrs. Gandhi's Congress came out victorious with thumping majority. It marked a total eclipse of the older leadership and a personal victory for Mrs. Gandhi.

This resulted in a new style of functioning in Indian politics. Democratic structures within the Congress were replaced by nominations from above, and the organizational culture of allowing democratic voices of dissent disappeared. The undemocratic elements in the Constitution were brought into extensive use. The normal institutional channels of dialogue and interaction were increasingly bypassed or subverted. There came into being a phase of repression leading to the rise of an authoritarian, executive centred system of governance and the emergence of new *modus operandi* of extracting mobilisational capacity of mass manipulation. "This, on the one hand, stiffled upward communication flows, and on the other, encouraged the ascendancy of bureaucracy.[5]

The bureaucracy was already powerful when India became independent. But initially it was obedient to the Congress rulers. But the waking influence of the Congress, the inner party squables and the necessity of firmly dealing with the masses brought the bureaucracy to the forefront

Almost at the beginning of 1970s India witnessed a phase of intensified political centralism. The newly emergent style of political management was characterized by a skilful combination of coercion, patronage and manipulation. The big bourgeoisie and the rich farmers began to grow immensely. In the case of top 20 industrial houses the growth was phenomenal : the value of their assets as recorded in 1969 increased by 25.9 per cent, 38.9 per cent, 61.3 per cent and 81.7 per cent in 1972, 1973, 1974 and 1975 respectively.[6] The green revolution augmented the income of the rich peasants.

Thus there developed an alliance between the big bourgeoisie, rich farmers and the party. From the middle of 1970s, however, the terms of trade grew unfavourably towards agriculture. This evoked discontent amongst the rich farmers which found its expression in the resolutions of the Akali Dal in Punjab. The agrarian discontent came to be spread to the many other parts of the country, especially those areas where capitalist development in agriculture took place and eventually led to rural mobilization. The ruling class perceived a threat to their rule, and opted for the Emergency to muzzle the voices of protest. An era of a highly centralized politics began in Indian politics. Care was also taken to prevent the possibility of the electorate from being alienated. To lend legitimacy to the actions of the state and to mobilize popular support such rhetorics as socialism, secularism and nationalism were frequently used.

But for a brief interlude during the Janata regime, the tradition of a centralized and executive-centred system of governance continued. Mrs. Gandhi's Congress came back to power in 1980. It resulted in a phase of politics of confrontation with low levels of legitimacy. In 1980s primordial loyalties came to be politicised. Hinduism that had been an 'artifact of categorization began to condition national consciousness. Hindu confessional politics became a form of what Rudolphs have called 'cultural nationalism for the Hindi Heartland States'[7]. Mrs. Gandhi's Congress openly courted Hindu support. This was evident in the Kashmir Assembly and Delhi municipal elections in 1983 when the voters who had traditionally voted for the Hindu-oriented Jan Sangh, supported Congress (I) candidates.

After coming back to power in 1980 Sikh extremism and terrorism in Punjab became an issue of national concern. In 1981 there took place what is popularly known as the Meenakshipuram conversions in which educated, prosperous untouchables converted to Islam in and around Meenakshipuram (Tamil Nadu) to win as Muslims the respect and equality which Hinduism denied. In Maharashtra and Gujarat where there are large scale concentrations of mostly poor Muslims, communal violence became endemic as a result of struggle between Hindus and Muslims over reservations, employment, property and business opportunities.

Mrs. Gandhi's attempt to recoup her party's position in Punjab by patronizing Sikh extremists resulted in a storm of communal politics. Bhindranwale was brought into political limelight to undermine the Akali Dal. He was chosen because he was the most uncompromising champion of Sikh fundamentalism with a following among the unemployed and underemployed youth. He was considered best fitted to embarrass the moderate and relatively affluent Akali leadership. From there it was a short step to rally support among the moderate Hindus by demonstrating the government's firmness against the 'extremists' demands in a manner that led many Rastriya Swayam Sevak Sangha (R.S.S). cadres to join the Congress in the 1984 elections. Her subsequent attempts to crush Sikh extremism by administrative measures worsened the situation. She was assassinated on October 31, 1984. The rise of confessional politics gave a very strong blow to the ideal of secularism India stood for. Kothari says that assassination represented a consummation of the culture of violence that had been prompted during the last years of Mrs. Gandhi. It also signalled an undermining of the many diversities that had structured the unity of India, and in the process, alienated large segments of population from the ruling elite.[8]

Rajiv Gandhi who succeeded Mrs. Gandhi carried forward the tradition of regional and confessional politics Mrs. Gandhi had initiated. His election campaign was based in part on Hindu backlash support, sympathy for a bereaved son whose mother had died as martyr to a Hindu cause and a campaign appeal for national unity. It was a time when the Muslims, the traditional vote bank of the Congress Party, were getting alienated. The Congress (I) Government in its desire to reverse the situation forced through the Muslim Women (Protection of Rights on Divorce) Bill 1986. It sought to establish the supremacy of the Muslim personal law as against the decision of the Supreme Court in Shah Bano case. It was an attempt to woo the Muslim voters. But he could not afford to ignore the Hindu votes. The Congress Party is reported to have sided wi.h Viswa Hindu Parishad on the question of the Babri Ramjanambhumi. The matter came to a head on the eve of the last elections, when the Rajiv Gandhi government seemed to have sided with the Viswa Hindu Parishad in laying the foundation stone of the Ramjanambhumi temple. The Rajiv Gandhi government had also played communal card in the North-Eastern States where the Christians are a majority.

Rajiv Gandh's regime witnessed anti-reservation compaigns. Starting with the 1972 elections the Congress Party increased the number of tickets it gave to persons from the backward classes, scheduled castes, tribals and muslims. This effort to shift the social base of the Congress party was evident in Karnataka and Andhra Pradesh, although it was also important in Maharashtra, Gujarat and Rajasthan. In Karnataka and Andhra Pradesh the percentage of reserved places for the backward classes in educational institutions and government services was increased. The forward castes rose in revolt in Gujarat, Andhra Pradesh, and Rajasthan.

Rajiv Gandhi's rule in India also witnessed the shifting of the agenda of the Indian state from one of socio-economic transformation to one of technological modernisation. Indian economy lost its self reliant character. Foreign indebtedness rose to an alarming height.

India's attempt at relatively autonomous development spearheaded by the state capitalist sector was looked with disfavour by the foreign agencies like the World Bank and the International Monetary Fund. They kept on putting pressure for a change in the overall economic policy of the Government in the direction of free play of the market forces. The liberalisation policy of the Rajiv Gandhi government under the rubric of New Economic Policy drew its inspiration from these agencies. The central thrusts in the policy were reduction of the role of the public sector, removal of variety of controls and licensing regulations, lowering of direct tax rates, a move towards more liberal imports etc. This new policy had disastrous consequences. The trade deficit which was 6060.75 crores in 1983-84 and Rs. 5390.5 crores in 1984-85, rose to Rs. 8747.5 crore in 1985-86.

The state during Rajiv Gandhi's regime seemed to have been fast losing its legitimacy. The threats to India's integrity from the bordering states, series of movements against the state, Kisan rallies in Delhi, strike all over the country etc., indicated the growing erosion of legitimacy of the state. The Rajiv Gandhi government attempted to deal with the problem in two ways. In the first place, it sought to utilize the police power of the state to tackle the problems of divisive forces. It also tried to regain legitimacy of the people by talking of revitalization of grassroots institutions.

The bourgeois-landlord alliance suffered strains and stresses during the regime of Rajiv Gandhi. At one point of time the party had enormous control over the rural votes. Things began to change since the days of Mrs. Gandhi. The emergence of rural vested interests has added a new dimension in Indian politics. This new rural lobby openly organised itself against the Congress (I) posing as the champion of ordinary peasants on demands like remunerative prices. The rise of Sharad Joshi in Maharashtra, of similar agitations in Gujarat and elsewhere and the Kisan morchas they have organised are signs that the most conservative section of Indian society are trying to shape country's policies.

The Rajiv Gandhi regime has given increased importance to bureaucracy. In the name of responsive administration the government attempted to enhance the prestige and image of the bureaucracy. It was reported in the newspapers that 10/15 bureaucrats led by R.K. Dhawan played significant role in the policy making processes. In fact, bureaucracy began to grow in strength when the Rajiv Gandhi government faced challenges from its party and when a number of scandals which the Press brought to light put his government to a very difficult position. The government took contradictory position. Rajiv Gandhi lalked of strengthening the bureaucracy and revitalization of grassroots institutions.

The general elections held in November, 1989 brought about a change in the government at the centre. The Congress (I) government was replaced by the National Front government led by an erstwhile Congressman, V.P. Singh. It is a minority government supported from outside by the left parties and Bhartiya Janta Party. It is difficult at this stage to comment on the performance of the government. It can, however, be said that this government has been trying to restore the democratic institutions, to reverse the process of centralization initiated by Mrs. Gandhi and to use the political channels of communication for entering into dialogue with the federating units. It has repealed some of the repressive legislations. It is true that its records so far is not impressive in matters of trackling the problems of divisive forces at the bordering states. It seems, however, determined to deal with the issues not only administratively, but also politically. It is also promise-bound to arrest the process of communalization of Indian polity and to set the bourgeois democratic house in India damaged by the Congress regimes in order.

REFERENCES

1. Charles Bettleheim, *India Independent*, Macgibbon and Kee, London, 1968, p. 5.

2. Javeed Alam, Class, Political and National Dimensions of State Autonomy Movements in India, in A Majeed (ed.) *Regionalism Developmental Dimensions in India*, Cosmo Publications, New Delhi, 1984, p. 46.

3. Federation of Indian Chambers of Commerce and Industry. *Proceedings of the 42nd Annual Session* (March 15-17, 1969, New Delhi) Kirloskar's Speech moving the "Resolution on National Integration and Business Community, p. 47.

4. *Ibid.*, G.M. Modi's Presidential Speech, p. 2.

5. Amal Ray, "From a Constitutional to an Authoritarian System of Government : 'Interactions between Politics and Constitutions in India' in the *Journal of Commonwealth and Comparative Politics*, (London) Volume XXV, No. 3, November 1987, p. 287.

6. S.K. Goyal, *Monopoly, Capital and Public Policy*, New Delhi, 1979, p. 53-58.

7. L.I. Rudolph and S.H. Rudolph, *In Pursuit of Lakshmi, The Political Economy of Indian State*. Orient Longman, New Delhi, 1987, p. 43.

8. R. Kothari, 'Whose India ?' *Seminar*, Annual, January, 1987, No. 329, p. 24.

CHAPTER 2

Rise of Regions in Indian Politics

Territory is the seat of politics. The Constitution provides for two seats of politics at the national and state levels. It makes room for another seat of politics at the local level. It does not, however block the emergence of new seats of powers as it provides for the creation of new territories under Article 3 of the Constitution. Politics in India as it began to unfold itself after Independence was essentially centrist because of the hegemonic influence of the Indian National Congress at the Centre as well as at the states. The winds of change began to blow from 1967 following the decline of the Congress and the rise of the regional parties. It led to what has been called regionalisation of Indian politics. The objective condition for the rise of a region as a seat of politics was created by the re-organisation of the territory in India in persuance with the States Re-organization Commission.

Defining Regionalism

Regions and regionalism are relative to the context or the parameters within which they are referred to and/or meaningfully operative. If African North of the Sahara South East Asia and Indian oceans are regions for certain purposes, and/or in a particular context, so are India, the different zones of the Indian Union, the Indian states, and even parts of the regions for different and definite reasons. Whatever be the context or parameters region may be said to connote an area, at least sufficiently large in size, which is differentiated or distinguishable from others by a variety of factors such as language, culture, religion etc. The International Encyclopedia of Social Sciences defines a region "as a homogeneous area with physical characteristics, distinct from those of neighbouring areas. As a part of the national domain a region is sufficiently unified to have consciousness of its customs and ideals, and thus possess a sense of identify distinct from the rest of the country. According to Webster's dictionary regionalism is nothing more than a consciousness of and loyalty to a distinct sub-national or supranational areas characterized by a common culture, background and interests. At the core of regionalism is a profound sense of identity of a group of people which is stronger than their identity with the nation or state. Regional identities may be based on geography, topography, religion, language, and customs, socio-economic and political stages of development, common historical tradition and experiences, a common way of living, and more than anything else, an evidently prevalent sentiment of togetherness. Regionalism may be a sort of political counter-movement meant for achieving greater autonomy for the region through greater degree of self government within the federal structure of the nation. Seligman thinks that it can be identified as "a counter movement to any exaggerated or oppressive form of centralization.[1] Regionalism can politically be understood "as a search for an intermediate control system between the centre and periphery for competitive advantages in the national arena."[2] In some cases, it is an assertion of its identity which is distinct from other culturally different regions (e.g., Samyukta Maharashtra movement). It may sometime turn towards separatism to fulfil political aspirations of a regional group living in that specific sub-cultural area (Vidarbha movement in Maharashtra). Regionalism may also manifest in the form of a movement for the special privileges for 'the sons of the soil' against outsiders (for example Shiv Sena movement in Maharashtra). It may also take the form of the demand for more powers for the states. One scholar has identified four different objects of regionalism in India, namely: (a) revival of the regional cultures, rebuilding of such cultural regions having distinctive identities within a nation; (b) administrative and political devolution; devising principles to solve centre-state confrontations between two or more sub-cultural regions; (c) to maintain economic and political equilibrium between the Centre and the States; nation and sub-cultural regions.[3]

Paradigmatic Framework

Broadly speaking, there are two major paradigms for explaining sub-national phenomenon in the post colonial third world countries. One is the pluralist theory which is rooted in the concept of modernization and the other is Marxian theory.

The pluralist theory seeks to explain regionalism with the help of the group theory. It seeks to connect the discontent of primordial groups in independent national states, as Geertz suggests to: (a) the new sense of political suffocation that arises when a nation state is formed with new, nationally organised institutions of civil power and influence and (b) the fact that these primordial groups and their members are not isolated from their own government centre of power, civil state as they were from the more remote colonial regime. He says that though primordial groups and loyalties are traditional and predate even colonial rule, primordial discontents are therefore movements based on these frustration and are very often only the result of independence and subsequent efforts at nation buildings.[4]

It is also argued that processes of modernisation, politicisation, participation, development, expanding education and media explosion within a democratic framework create a sense of self-awareness and sharpen edge for identities based on region. The ethnic groups acquire an added importance as they fill a vacuum created by the decline of institutions. Modern technology and knowledge have increased mobilizational potential of primordial loyalties faster than that of the political parties and other modern institutions.[5]

There is another group of scholars basically grounded in Marxian analysis who seek to examine regional phenomenon in the post colonial third world countries essentially in the light of the problem of nationalities and the path of development the country has treaded. The Marxists argue that primordial loyalties which constitute some of the key sources of regionalism, are rooted in pre-capitalist relations of production. In the post-colonial third world countries capitalism coexists with feudalism, and this constitutes the breeding ground of primordial loyalties.

Typologies of Regionalism

Iqbal Narain has tried to draw a typology of regionalism in

India taking the state as the unit of analysis,[6] although regionalism is not always coterminus with present day state boundaries. He has identified three types of regionalism in India, namely, supra-state regionalism, inter-state regionalism and inter-state regionalism. Supra-state regionalism is built around, and is an expression of group identity of several states which get together and take a common stand on an issue of mutual interest vis-a-vis another group of states or the Central Government. Inter-state regionalism is coterminus with the state boundaries, and involve juxtaposing of one or more identities against another on specific issues. Finally, there is the phenomenon of inter-state regionalism. It embodies a quest of a part within a state for self identity and self development. Iqbal Narain's typology is based on form rather than on content.

Vanaik suggests that regionalism in India is two dimensional. On the one hand, there are regional pressures and sub-national movements the area of operation of which coincides with the federal territorial division of the union into different states. In this category is included centre-state and inter-state conflicts. In these cases the state government plays the most crucial role. On the other hand, there are the sub-state pressures and movements which are directed against the state government, or the centre or both. These regional movements combine popular grievances from below with elements of manipulation from above. The leadership of such regional movements seek to institutionalize its own political authority and through this, eventually accumulate wealth, and become part of the regional bourgeoisie.[7] Such movements seem to have been very powerful when economic issues are fused with cultural grievances.[8] The sub-state movements usually aim, if not at attaining power at the state level (this was the goal of the Assam Agitation), then at achieving some degree of political autonomy like statehood or autonomous council status (Gorkhaland). Such movements are primarily seen in tribal regions as in Jharkhand. These movements have populist overtones and take agitational form. These movements have also fluctuating intensities.

The Central Issues

Thus there are two major phenomenal forms of regionalism in India. One is the growing assertiveness of the states expressed in the form of more powers for the states or sharing of resources between states. The state here is the unit. The empirical referent of another from of regionalism is sub-state (Bodo Agitation in Assam) or covering more than one state (Jharkhand Agitation for a separate state). This may be designated as ethnic regionalism. Clearly, in the first form the state is the actor and issues relate to sharing of resources. In the second form the ethnic groups are the actors.

The Centre-State struggles are more institutionalized in character. Inter-state conflicts are primarily focused on economic and political, not cultural issues. Broadly speaking they are the by-products of uneven regional development.

There are also inter-state migrations of labour which give rise to 'sons of the soil movements' for restricting employment to local state residents. The agrarian bourgeoisie generally welcomes migrant rural labour as it helps to push wage rate down. Interestingly, most imortant 'sons of the soil' movements have been urban-based. The most powerful such movements were launched by Shiv Sena in Bombay, Maharashtra and the Kannada Chaluvaligars in Bangalore, Karnataka, All Assam Students' Union in Assam etc.

The Centre-State struggles are confined to the domain of political and economic decentralization. States want more powers to legislate on issues concerning them. As the governor is an agent of the Centre at the state, the state governments want say in matters of appointment/nomination of governors. The all India bureaucracy posted at the state level is answerable to the Centre. Some states like the Left Front-ruled West Bengal has demanded separate recruitment and control over all India bureaucracy.

Above economic matters, the state governments want more freedom from interference and control ever the state plans by the Central Planning Commission. They want more licensing powers concerning industry, commerce, energy projects. The states are unhappy with their share of taxes and levies collected by the Centre. The states would like the statutory component of compulsory disbursement by the Centre to increase substantially. The Centre has become very powerful today because of numerous additional amendments giving it more powers to intervene through various repressive measures. After the deinstitutionalization of the Congress and the rise of regional parties, the Congress Government at the Centre found it difficult to cope with centrifugal forces and resorted to repression.

The scholars like Javeed Alam look at the demand of the states for more powers as the product of the centralisation of powers which is rooted in the path of development the ruling classes in India have been pursuing since Independence. The ruling classes in India have all along sought to develop India along the capitalist lines. The development of capitalism necessitates as one of its conditions the formation of the larger markets for commodity production. This necessity plus the requirements of the big capital demand growing centralization.

It is also to be mentioned that there is a political aspect of this centralization, namely uninterrupted rule of the Congress Party for the first thirty years both at the Centre and in most of the states, and was necessitated due to the rowing challenge to the hegemony of the Congress rule which began to surface since 1967. Javeed Alam writes, "Behined the Congress nanoeuvres were the desperate moves of an insecure bourgeoisie in face of the mounting crisis of the capitalist path of development."[9]

Inter-State Disputes

Confrontations between states principally centre round the issues relating to boundaries, river water, irrigation, location of power projects, language etc.[10] Important border disputes are between Maharashtra and Karnataka over the Belgaum district, Punjab and Haryana over Chandigarh, Andhra and Orissa over the Durramutha and twelve other villages lying in an enclave within some taluka of Vishakhapatnam district. Major inter-state disputes, however, relate to resource sharing such as river water. The dispute over the water of river Narmada among Madhya Pradesh, Gujarat, Maharashtra, and Rajasthan over the utilization of power of Krishna and Godavari rivers among states of Maharashtra, Karnataka and Andhra Pradesh are important examples. Similar other disputes among states over resource sharing relate to the construction and ownership of the dam over the tributary Ravi among the states of Punjab, Jammu & Kashmir, Haryana and Himachal Pradesh. Some of these disputes owe their origin to the constitutional ambivalence of the states, while others to role of the Centres. The role of the Centre in the inter-state discords becomes apparent when it is moved by partisan considerations in locating industrial projects or supplying and distributing essential items.

Ethno-regionalism

Some of the ethnic groups in India seem to be very restive today. India is a multinational country with pluralities of culture. It is a country of continental proportion with a distinct history and a heavy colonial hangover. The colonial rulers used ethnic groups as pawns in the power game. They retained power by creating a divide among the ethnic groups. India's effort to provide a political framework for cultural pluralities seems to have failed to yield desired results. The project of transforming ethnic identities into a national identity of citizens is now subject to centrifugal ethnic pulls in the society. Some ethnic minorities seem to feel more insecure. Some of them are demanding an autonomous political arrangement for themselves, some of them within a particular state (the Bodos in Assam for example), some others spreading over more than one state (the Jharkhandis, for example) and a few of them outside the Indian Union (the Nagas, Mizos, for example).

Ethnic regionalism is the product of the precapitalist survivals and weak or more or less dependent capitalism. The stagnant economy, massive poverty, unemployment and less free political milieu are often deflected on to ethnic disturbances. Persistence of uneven development of economy and society and neo-colonial domination breeds movement of the backward and oppressed nationalities. In India, there is no single oppressing nationality. Individuals from the different nationalities dominate various parts of the country.[11] The all-India bourgeoisie for its own interest require an all-India centralized market and freedom to exploit raw materials and labour of all nationalities. Thus, they oppose the right of every nationality and ethnic group to have an equal opportunity in economic growth and cultural development. The local bourgeoisie on the other hand, tend to mobilize people against the other dominant cultural and linguistic groups. The rich peasantry also mobilize the masses on ethnic lines for their own advantage. The problem or regional chauvinism in all its manifestations after India became Independent has its roots in the betrayal by the big bourgeoisie at the time of transfer of power in 1947.[12] In the course of the freedom struggle the attitude of the bourgeoisie to nationality aspiration was vascillating, and it showed a compromising approach to fedual ideology.[13]

The Attitude of the Indian National Congress to the Aspirations of the Nationalities

During the days of the freedom movement the Indian National Congress lent its support to the linguistic nationality principle by opposing the partition of Bengal and supporting its annulment. The issue came up before the Calcutta Congress Session in 1917 as a sequal to the Andhradesha movement in 1913. It generated a lot of heat, and by 1918 Gandhiji accepted the logic in favour of the linguistic provinces. The Nagpur Session of the Congress held in 1920 gave the idea a concrete shape taking a resolution to reorganise the Pradesh Congress Committees on a linguistic basis. It was certainly an organizational innovation which laid stress on homogeneous linguistic units ignoring the existing administrative demarcation of provinces in accordance with the colonial policy. The Provincial Congress Committees played very important role in organizing movements. It was also an important forum for the Congress leaders to assert their control over the organization of the national movement throughout the country. The significance of language as a principle for provincial re-organization was further accepted in the Calcutta Session in 1937. The Motilal Nehru Report extended its support and the All Parties Conference held in 1928 endorsed the Nehru Committee's recommendations. The 1945-46 election manifesto of the Congress Party committed itself to linguistic re-organization if it was voted to power.

The Gap Between the Promise and Performance : The Constituent Assembly Phase

During the formation of the Constituent Assembly a Commission was set up with Justice Dar as Chairman to examine the issue. It was suggested : "The formation of provinces exclusively, or even mainly on linguistic considerations is not in the larger interest of the Indian nation, and should not be taken in hand". Clearly, the concept of Indian nation had been the moving spirit behind the Report.

The recommendations of the Committee were not received well by all sections of the Congressmen especially from the non-Hindi areas. And as a sequel to a petition to the working committee to reconsider the issue came a three-membered committee consisting of Nehru, Patel and Sitaramayya. The Report of the Committee could not endorse the linguistic principle for provincial re-organization although it found strong points in favour of the demand of Andhra. It accorded its approval to the demand for a separate Andhra State.

This was followed by the constitution-making exercise. It became easier now on the part of founding fathers to refuse to take any concrete decision on the linguistic re-organization of states with the Dar Commission report in their hands. The trauma of partition provided further support. One scholar has explained it thus : "the temper of radicalism roused by the mass struggles for Independence, the struggle in Telengana and partition made Nehru and Congress leadership reject the linguistic nationality question."[14] The Assembly listed 14 national languages in the Eighth Schedule, but maintained a meaningful silence in matters of re-organization of provinces. Hindi was made official language by 1965. But no provision was made for encouraging the regional languages to enable them to occupy their rightful place in the nationality regions.[15] Thus neither the transfer of power nor the framing of new India's Constitution could resolve the problem of linguistic nationality. Clearly Independence did not pave the road for the growth of the emerging nationalities. It was the ghost of India as a nation which haunted the minds of the architects of 'new' India. Thus the retarded growth of nationalities continued unabated even after Independence.

The Constitution of the States Re-organization Committee

The refusal by the Constitution makers to recognize the principle of linguistic nationality caused consternation and discontent among the Congressmen at the provincial level. The Vishalandhra Movement gathered immense momentum during the late forties. The death of a vateran Gandhian, Potti Sriramulu out of a long drawn fast caused widespread unrest throughout Andhra. In 1952 Nehru announced the formation of Andhra. This decision stimulated the demand for the re-organization of states in India, especially in the southern part of the country as an offshoot of which came the States Reorganization Commission (SRC) in 1953.

The Rise of Regional Elites

The SRC Report generally accepted the linguistic principle. The major phase of linguistic reorganization was accomplished by the end of the fifties. But linguistic re-organization by itself was no panacea to the ills of retarted growth of nationalities. The principle of the matter remained to be resolved. The Indian state had always taken the position that there was only one nation—India. The creation of linguistic states strengthened the hands of the regional bourgeoisie and rich peasants. They began to establish close ties with the dominant linguistic, communal and caste groups in order to strengthen and consolidate their position in the field of decision-making and power politics at the provincial level. This resulted in a shift in country's political life from an all-India to regional orientation facilitating the trend towards regionalisation of Indian politics.

Highly Centralized Federal Form of Government

Indian nationalism had two features. It was pan-Indian and regional for the successful fruition of the twin processes of this sort of nationalism there was a need for a truely 'federal' form of government. But unfortunately the ubiquitous 1935 Act which had served colonial interests was chosen as the model for dealing with centre-state matters. India adopted a highly centralized model of government. It was pointed out by Dr. Ambedkar in the Constituent Assembly while moving the draft constitution that conditions in the modern world were such that centralization of power was inevitable. It may be recalled that the draft constitution prepared by the constitutional advisers proposed that the country should be called the 'Federation of India'. But the proposal was rejected. It was rephrased as "India that is Bharat shall be a union of states". The most elastic sources of taxes were given to the Union Government. The dependence of the states for resources has been alarmingly growing over the years. The rise of dependence is consistent. The situation becomes abundantly clear if we take into account the loan component from the institutions under the control of the Central Government. The aggregate transfer as percentage of aggregate expenditure of states increased consistently from 37.8% during the First Plan to 47.4%, during the Fourth Plan. It declined during the Fifth and Sixth Plan and was around 42%. Such a 'weak' state can hardly afford to meet the requirements and aspirations of the nationalities.

Whatever be the rationale for this overcentralization the fact remains that the state governments are hard pressed to meet the ever increasing demands for the socio-economic upliftment of the people as their resources are very limited and the tax base is extremely narrow. The process of centralization rooted in the Constitution received a boost following the hegemonic rule of the Congress Party at the Centre and at the States.

The 1967 general elections broke the domination of the Congress. The need for review of centre-state relations was first formally suggested by the Rajamannar Committee appointed by the Karunanidhi Government of Madras in 1969. The demand for state autonomy gathered ground after the emergence of the Janata Party at the Centre. The non-Janata Chief Ministers and political leaders attempted to create public opinion in favour of the demand for state autonomy. This led to the setting up of the Sarkaria Commission in 1983 the report of which has been submitted. It is the multinationality of India which constitutes the basis for the demand of state outonomy to which the Commission does not seem to have given due attention.

Regional Imbalance : Past and Present

Colonial economic development was very insignificant and concentrated chiefly around the Presidency towns to which the rest of the country served as hinterland. Capitalist growth in India after Independence has shown a strong tendency towards self-perpetuating unevenness both region-wise and community-wise. The uneven development of capitalism led to regional concentration of industrial development. The Hazari Report on Industrial Planning and Licensing Policy, 1967 pointed out that most of Marwari, Gujrati and Parsi investment was concentrated in three states of Maharashtra, West Bengal and Madras.[16] Such outcomes are evident in other fields too.

Regional differences in the field of agriculture were deliberately promoted by colonial rulers. During the colonial period government policy with respect to land settlement and the extent of commercial penetration into the agricultural economy differed from region to region. The eastern states were the major contributors to the colonial exchequer. And it was with a view to stabilizing the colonial revenues that the imperial rulers introduced the zamindari system of land tenure in the eastern part of India.

By contrast, the western region, comprising the present Punjab, Haryana and western Uttar Pradesh as well as the coastal Andhra and Tamil Nadu was characterized by a terminal system based on proprietorship. This region benefitted from massive public investments in irrigation. These regional differences in tenurial conditions along with the irrigation policy of the government resulted in the emergence of 'small enclaves of growth' and vast areas of low productivity and stagnation.[17]

It is true that we should not expect even rates of growth in the field of agriculture because of time-variant region-effects, like the types of soil, and natural endowments. But there is no justification for abysmal regional disparities most of which have been accentuated by technological and institutional factors. The strategy of 'Green Revolution' was a growth strategy which led to the emergence of a few pockets of growth. The JNUPPD study showed that growth rates of agricultural output higher than 5% were experienced in approximately 12% of the districts in the country between triennium 1963-66 and the teriennium 1970-73. These districts accounted for 14% of gross cropped area but consumed 20% of major inputs.[18]

In terms of value of agricultural output per hectare (1970's) this study identified three cores of high productivity viz., (i) Ganganagam Punjab-Haryana Western UP, (ii) Deltaic West Bengal and its projection into Central Bihar along the Ganga, and (iii) the coastal plains of Andhra, Tamil Nadu, Kerala and Karnataka. These cores are skired by medium-productivity regions. In terms of productivity per acre the areas of high productivity shrink and include only Punjab, Haryana and Western UP. Clearly the 'Green Revolution' has led to the accentuation of the process of regional disparities.

The talks of multi-level planning as a measure for removing regional disparities were heard during the Fourth Five Year Plan period. The Task Force on Multi-level Planning and Spatial Analysis was also appointed in 1972. But no remarkable progress is in sight. Regionalisation of the country for this purpose is yet to be done. The states constitute an important level of regional planning, but most of them are yet to develop their effective planning instruments. Regional planning is not mere physical planning, but includes integrated and coordinated planning between physical, economic and social components in a given region. It has been rightly said : 'The crux of the problem is that the objective of balanced regional development is sought to be pursued under a highly inequitous system of private ownership of the means of production, distribution and exchange along with the colonial heritage of regional disparities.''[19]

Regional imbalances are producing both prosperity and poverty between regions. Within the regions they are also giving rise to the birth of two classes rich and poor. Take for example, the case of Punjab. The Punjab economy recorded a very high rate of growth during the sixties as a result of the 'Green Revolution'. It also resulted in uneven development in different regions of the state. The fruits of the 'Green Revolution' have been grabbed by just 20% of jat rich farmers who own more than 60% of the total land.[20] It is this group of prosperous peasants who sought commanding positions in the Akali Dal as they were keen to match their economic muscle with political power. On the contrary, the number of landless became doubled, and that of the marginal peasants increased three times in ten years.[21] With capital intensive agriculture the percentage of landless workers in the total agricultural work force rose from 17.3% in 1961 to 32% in 1971. According to Bhalla 24% of the small peasants and 81% of marginal peasants live below the poverty line.[22]

Thus, the 'Green Revolution' has increased prosperity of the land owing class and caused growing frustration among the large army of the landless and marginal farmers. The prosperous class became also frustrated when they found themselves trapped in the nexus of capitalist market economy. It is their frustration which contributes to the development of alienation among them from the mainstream and a lust for separation.

Role of Finance and Planning Commission

The Constitution of India has provided for the appointment of Finance Commission to examine and recommend on the problems arising out of economic imbalance between the expenditures and resources of the state government. But the ninth Finance Commission that have so far been appointed, have failed to bring about desired results. It does not seem to have ever taken into account the question of regional economic inequalities while considering fund allocation to the states. The Planning Commission enjoys more powers than the Finance Commission in recommending resource transfer from the Centre to the states. The aggregate budgetary transfers show that they have not served the equity goals. A study of inter-state distribution of certain identifiable central plan outlays over the first thirty years of planning reveals that equity has not been a predominant objective of central plan expenditure. This is evident from the central per capita plan outlay received by low income states like Uttar Pradesh and Rajasthan. It is found that the per capita state plan expenditure has been low in states with low per capita income and high in states with high per capita income. Incidentally equity consideration is also the least important objective in the inter-state distribution of investment fund by specialised financial institutions as also working capital funds by commercial banks[23].

The Capitalist Path of Development

Independence raised the hopes of nationalities and created among them what may be called a revolution of rising expectations. But India adopted capitalist path of development. Capitalism was then not only a moribund force all over the world but in the third world its growth and expansion has further been marked by retardation and distortions. It has resulted in the perpetuation of pre-capitalist social divisions. Capitalism does not in the third world unify and amalgamate the people, but generates separatist tendencies and aspirations. The growing capitalism in the period of the genesis and consolidation of European nation states could break all barrier to its expansion. But the third world capitalism is incapable of creating new social unity after destroying the precapitalist forms because of its colonial past when it developed along with pre-capitalist forces and the socio-economic background of the ruling classes.

The growing contradictions of capitalism have revealed themselves in the form of the growth of monopolies, concentration of wealth in the hands of a few along with the rise of unemployment, poverty, increase in wage erosion etc. The contradictions of capitalist development are obliging the state to play a more positive role in the management of crisis, requiring more and more centralization of powers.[21] This is causing a sense of frustration and alienation from the national mainstream amongst the nationalities often taking the shape of hostile reaction.

Manipulative Politics and its Implications

Added to all these is the rise of manipulative politics in India since the days of Mrs. Gandhi. She had to shield herself against many attacks when she took over the party as President and the Government as Prime Minister. This was how the era of manipulative politics dawned in Indian scene in different forms. It is now widely acknowledged that it was she who contributed largely to the rise and growth of Bhindranwale in Punjab politics. She brought him into limelight to counter the growing popularity of the Akali Dal. She did not care to consider sympathetically some of the legitimate demands of the Akali Dal as it did not fit in well with her design of larger politics. After some initial trouble she could stop the dissident voices in the party and to collect around her a fairly large band of loyalists, and thus, to tide over the crisis. The Congress party at the Centre after Mrs. Gandhi's death was caught in the vortex of a deeper crisis as was evident from the rising tide of dissidence within the party, the growing erosion of support base and the steady loss of face of the party before the public as a sequel to the disclosure of many unfair practices in the public deals such as Bofors. When the Rajiv Gandhi Government was installed at the Centre the ruling party had been in power in 18 states. The party lost power in 6 states after he took over. The edifice, the Hindi heartland, which had for long been the support base of the party crumbled. All these seemed to have compelled the ruling party to play discriminatory, manipulative politics in a cruder form and on more frequent occasions leading to discontent, frustration and alienation amongst a section of some of the nationalities The present upsurge of the separatist movements in some parts of North-East India, and Jharkhand, received its immediate stimulus from the concession of the demand for separate statehood in some parts of North-Eastern India. The primary spark that touched off the Gorkhaland conflagration in Darjeeling was the eviction of thousands of Nepalis from Meghalaya in February 1986. It is strange that the outlawed organizations like Mizo National Front were prima facie, legitimised by the Central Government by inviting them to dialogue and by allowing them to sign what is called Peace Accords. This enthused the separatist forces and gave ethnic nationalities in some parts of the country an impetus to organise themselves for launching struggle.

The Role of the Foreign Powers

The national question has become the happy hunting ground of world imperialism today. The ascendancy of the Reagan Administration marked an intensification of the imperialist attempts for global hegemony manifested in the U.S. strategy of confrontation with the Soviet Union at many levels. He stated that the security of "our countries is indivisible, and must be approached on a global basis."[25]

India occupies a place of importance in the context of the U.S. global strategy. India is one of the major developing countries and a substantial regional power in the South and South West Asian region. India again does not share U.S. perception of its vital interests in the region as reflected in the orientation and direction of the Non-Aligned Movement, declaration of Indian Ocean as a zone of peace etc.

In the last few years imperialist agencies and forces have been found active to influence the course of development in the third world countries through a variety of tactics and instruments. For example, a large number of voluntary agencies and action groups funded by the foreign agencies are at work among the rural poor, tribals, women and unorganised labour in India. According to one scholar a large number of these voluntary agencies and action groups, which together received funds exceeeding Rs. 200 million annually from governments and foundations of Western capitalist countries, have become important conduits for imperialist penetration.[26] They have been capitalizing on the growing frustrations which have been gaining ground among the nationalities as a result of the failure of the economic and political system to generate an atmosphere conducive to their healthy growth.

The imperialist organs and agencies have been helping separatist and secessionist movements in the North-East and North-West of India. The widely known Himalayan Border Studies Project and more recent Project Brahmaputra financed by the U.S. Central Intelligence Agency were designed to study ethnic tensions and identify and encourage separatist elements in West Bengal, Assam and Tripura.

The ideological impetus and financial support for a separate Sikh state was provided by certain affluent members of the Sikh Community in foreign countries.[27] The major organisations pleading for Khalistan are the National Council of Khalistan, Dal Khalsa, Babbar Khalsa which operate in U.K., Germany, Canada and U.S.A. There is evidence of close links between the US CIA and the Sikh extremists. For example, the extremists forged ties with the Rightwing Senator Helms who has close links with CIA and Graham, the former Chief of Defence Intelligence Agency.[28] Until recently the BBC allowed Chauhan to use its broadcasting network for publicising the Khalistan cause.

Conditions of Regionalism : Objective and Subjective

It is evident from the above discussion that there are two main components of regionalism, namely, the factors of regional awareness and the conditions for the articulation of this awareness. Ziauddin Khan calls them objective and subjective. The objective component includes territory along with physical and manmade environment. The subjective components are ways of living, customs and traditions, language and literature, social heritage etc.[29] Thus the first comprises demographic specificities based on geographical, economic and socio-cultural variations. The diversity of physical features and climatic conditions create a conducive atmosphere for the growth of natural regions. The variant geographical conditions have made a profound impact on the economic life of the people. It wielded them into distinct socio-cultural groups based on language, customs, practices etc. The cultural landscape of the country was further fragmented as a result of influx of alien ethnic groups from time to time. The rise of the British rule brought in its wake a rapid centralization of powers and its subsequent delegation to the regional middle classes in the form of local self government and provincial autonomy. It had rigidified and federalized the Indian polity in a different manner. The new alignment took place along linguistic lines, because the linguistic middle classes emerged on the scene following the extension of administration to remote areas of land and consequent induction of large masses in the administrative and other infrastructures. The British rulers sought to satisfy the linguistic groups within the colonial limits by re-organizing administrative units.[30]

These factors of regional consciousness could not provide the objective basis for regionalism under the pre-colonial and colonial conditions. These were counteracted by the strong general features of the Indian social structure, such as, single dominant religions system, an all pervasive caste system etc. The colonial exploitation led to the political consolidation of the country. Colonial rule created a national market and built a centralized state structure. Thus it unified the various ethnic groups and developing nationalities. In essence, this proved to be the greatest obstacle to the development of individual nationalities.[31] The nationalities were divided into various administrative units. The impact of colonial integration and centralized control varied from regions to regions. The unified Indian national state emerged out of all India movement waged a battle by all the linguistic groups against the British imperialism. Alongside this there developed nascent linguistic nationality consciousness of the different nationalities. Clearly, the twin process began to operate at two levels. Thus Indian nationalism was both Pan-Indian and regional. In the struggle for independence these two forces combined against the common enemy—the British imperialism.

The post colonial India created conditions for the growth of regionalism by releasing the forces of bourgeois democracy and capitalism. The transfer of political power meant disappearence of the common enemy leading to the erosion of the subjective basis of national unity. The Indian National Congress to whom the power was transferred betrayed the nationalities by abondoning the federal principle and compromising with landlordism. India opted for the capitalist path which has its inherent limitations. The growing aspirations of the nationalities as a result of the Independence remained unfulfilled because of the backward and dependent nature of our capatalism. The feudal ideology was allowed to have its play because of the compromise. The political process that the Indian state generated led to its accentuation. The ruling classes began to manipulate the primordial loyalties for its stay on in power. All these provided a conducive atmosphere for the rise of the regional forces.

The politics of subnationalism has created a dilemma for

the state. A 'strong' state response may generate more extremism and resistance. A 'weak' state response may invite further mobilizations that challenge a state whose legitimacy and capabilities have been in decline sence the mid 1970s.[32]

Concluding Observations

The conventional theories of development are insensitive to regional demands and aspirations. Regionalism is used by the ruling classes in a pejorative sense. It is regarded as a divisive trend detrimental to national unity. In popular parlance it is supposed to be synonym of provincialism which breeds localism, isolationism and separatism. It is dangerous when it is manipulated by the ruling classes to disrupt the unity of the working classes. In that case regionalism gets converted into regional chauvinism. But regionalism has a progessive dimension which reflects democratic awakening of the linguistic nationality consciousness and a struggle for equality and balanced development of all nationalities. The liberal pluralists would argue that the multiplicity of intermediary loyalties can strengthen nationalism in a number of ways. For them subnational identities are natural phenomena in a democratic society and are also a surest guarantee against political conformism and regimentation. Puri feels that there are three positive aspects of regionalism. In the first place, it provides for full growth of the human personality which singular loyalty cannot do. Secondly, it provides an emotional link between the individual and the nation. Thirdly, multiple loyalties act as checks on each other and help a person to outgrow parochial and limited loyalties.[33] Regional movements play positive role when they help in arriving at a democratic solution of the problem of nationalities in a multinational country like ours. When some states get together and ask for more powers of the states it has a positive side because it seeks to solve the basic problem of nationalities. But as Alam suggest, it loses its progressive edge when the regional bourgeoisie and landed rich clamour for more powers. Thus the demand for more powers of the state has to be examined against the background of the classroots and class needs of the ruling parties. For example, the parties like ADMK and Akali Dal represent specific interests of the ruling classes within their states. It is, therefore, likely that they would clamour for more powers for statgs in the interest of the locally placed ruling class groups at a time when their interests are not best served by the centralized state. The left democratic parties on the other hand, need real state autonomy in the interest of democratic economy and democratic polity. The left democratic concept of state autonomy, poses a a challenge to the structure of state power itself.

REFERENCES

1. R.A. Seligman and Johnson, *Encyclopedia of Social Sciences*, Allen & Unwin, London, pp. 208-209.

2. Jyotirindra Dasgupta, 'Nation, Region and Welfare : Ethnicity, Regionalism and Development Politics in South Asia' in *Annals*, AAPSS, September, 1977, p. 132.

3. Arun K. Chatterjee, 'Sociological Context of Regionalism in India : A Conceptual Framework' in Satish Chandra et al, (ed) *Regionalism and National Integration.*, Alekh, Jaipur, 1977, pp. 31-32.

4. C. Geertz, 'The Integrative Revolution' in C. Geertz (ed.), *Old Societies and New States*, Amerind Publications, 1971.

5. Balraj Puri, 'Politics of Ethnic and Communal Identities', *Economic and Political Weekly*, April 7, 1990.

6. Iqbal Narain, Regionalism in India : A Conceptual Framework in A Majeed, (ed.) *Regional Development Tensions in India*, Cosmos, 1984.

7. Achin Vanaik, 'Is There a Nationality Question in India ?' *Economic and Political Weekly*, October 29, 1988.

8. R. Hardgrave (Jr.), 'The North East, Punjab and Regionalization of Indian Politics', *Asian Survey*, November, 1983, p. 171.

9. Javeed Alam, 'Class, Political and National Dimensions of State Autonomy Movements in India' in Aktar Majeed (ed.) *Regional Development Dimensions in India*, Cosmo Publications, 1984.

10 For details, see, S R. Maheshwari, "Inter-state Discords in State Policy in India", *Indian Journal of Political Science*, October-December, 1987.

11. Ajit Roy, 'Some Aspects of the National Question in India' *Marxisi Review*, 1967.

12. R. Ulyanovosly & V. Pavlov, The Asia and African Countries : Specific Features of Development, *Social Sciences*, No. 4, 1980.

13. Prakash Karat, 'Problems of National Unity : Historical and Economic Roots of Regionalism' *Social Scientist*, September, 1984, p. 57.

14. Karat, P., *Language and Nationality Politics in India*, Orient Longman Limited, Madras, 1973, p. 35.

15. See for details, G. Austin., '*The Indian Constitution* : *Cornerstone of a Nation*, Oxford University Press, London, 1966.

16. R K. Hazari, *Industrial Planning and Licensing Policy*, Government of India, New Delhi, 1967, p. 4, para 2.

17. K. Subbarao, 'State Policies and Regional Disparity in Indian Agriculture', *Development and Change*, Vol. 16, 1986.

18. G.S. Bhalla and Y.K. Alagh, *Performance of Agriculture*, Sterling, New Delhi, 1979.

19. A.G. Minocha, 'Regional Disparities in India'. 'Some Basic Issues', Social Scientist, May, 1983, p. 56.

20. H K. Puri, 'Socio-Political Bases of Akali Agitation' *EPW*, January, 22, 1983, p. 116.

21. G.S. Bhalla, *et. al*, Structural Analysis of Gujarat, Punjab and Haryana Economics, New Delhi, 1980, p. 144.

22. G.S. Bhalla, and Y.K. Alagh, "Green Revolution and Small Peasants. A Study of Income Distribution in Punjab Agriculture", *EPW*. May 22, 1982, p. 876.

23. R.V. Dadibhavi, 'Why These Inter-State Disparities', *Yojana*, Vol. 31, No. 11.

24. G. Singh, "Regionalism in India Political Culture", *Calcutta Journal of Political Studies*, Summer, 1983, p 28.

25. Quoted in H.S. Surjeet, 'The International Situation' *The Marxist*, October-December, 1983.

26. P. Karat, 'Action Groups/Voluntary Organizations : A Factor in Imperialist Strategy, *The Maxist*, April-June, 1984.

27. See *White Paper on Punjab Agitation*, Government of India, New Delhi, 1984.

28. *India Today*, December 15, 1984.

29. Ziauddin Khan, *National Integration in India : Issues and Dimensions*, Associated Publishing, New Delhi, 1983, p. 15.

30. Konsar J Azam, *Political Aspects of National Integration,* Meenakshi Prakashan, New Delhi, 1987.

31. E M.S Namboodripad, *The National Question in Kerala,* Peoples Publishing House, Bombay, 1952, p. 60.

32. S.J. Rudolph, and S.H. Rudolph, In Pursuit of Lakshmi : The Political Economy of the Indian State, Orient Longman, 1987, p. 3.

33. Balraj Puri, 'Subnational Identities and National Integration' *Economic and Political Weekly,* June 26, 1976, p. 945.

CHAPTER 3

Political Environment of India's Federalism

Federalism as an intergovernmental arrangement is an extension of democracy on a territorial plane. The experience of success of federal form of government in the West demonstrates that it can develop in an atmosphere of relatively homogeneous social order and in a tradition of democratic value and spirit. Wheare says that it is appropriate for a group of states which desire to be united, but not to be unitary.[1] The third world countries like India have a long colonial tradition which itself retaveds the growth of the federal plant. In our country the rise of a federal system has a peculiar background. India under the British rule had evolved a governing tradition which suited the colonial interests. For example, princely states were created by the imperialists to consolidate the colonial empire. This background has to be kept in mind while considering the question of centre-state relations in India.

This chapter seeks to analyse the changing political environment of India's federalism. It is the contention of the chapter that the process of centralization which has vitiated the federal environment in the country has been facilitated by the more or less uninterrupted Congress rule both at the Centre and in most of the States for about three decades and has been necessitated by the class needs and power structure of the ruling party, and the path of development the country has chosen.

Federalism and the Freedom Movement

The idea of forming a federal system of Government in India came to be posed before the freedom movement since the early days of the century. It was a time when two parallel movements led by the Congress, on the one hand, and the Muslim League, on the other, dominated the political scene. The idea received a sharp focus in the Lucknow Pact between the Congress and the Muslim League in 1916. Two contradictory pulls had been at work since then. The leaders of the Congress and the Liberal Party fought for the maximum amount of centralization, and the League worked for the best possible decentralization. In this 'unitary versus federal' controversy the issue of demarcation of powers came to be hotly debated, and sharp differences of opinion between the Congress and the League over the question of residuary powers came to the limelight. The All Parties Committee headed by Pt. Motilal Nehru, the Round Table Conference and the Committee set up by them and all subsequent negotiations leading to the Cabinet Mission Plan had debated the issue. The Congress and the liberal parties went on making compromise after compromise to avoid partition of the country.

The Birth of a Partitioned India

But India that emerged on August 15, 1947, was a partitioned

India. Immediately after partition Nehru spoke of the need for 'a strong centre with a federal structure.' To quote him "Now that partition is a settled fact, we are unanimously of the view that it would be injurious to the interests of the country to provide for a weak central authority which would be incapable of ensuring peace, of coordinating vital matters of common concern, and of speaking effectively for the whole country in the international sphere. At the same time we are quite clear in our minds that there are many matters in which authority must rest solely with the unit, and that to frame our Constitution on the basis of a unitary state would be a retrograde step, both politically and administratively.[2]" It has to be kept in mind that there was no compulsion of an organised political force like the Muslim League to compel the founding fathers of the Indian Constitution to adhere to the framework already laid down. The result was, as E.M.S. Namboodripad says, "while the superficial structure of a federal constitution remained, it was hedged in by innumerable provisions which could make it possible for a strong ruling party dominant at the centre to make inroads into the powers of the federating units and transform the constitution into a unitary one, while it appeared to be unitary."[3]

Federalism : The Phase of One Party Dominance

Indian federalism began in an atmosphere of one party dominance at the central and regional levels and hierarchically structured party organisation with Nehru occupying the Centre of authority. There were certainly differences and conflicts between the Centre and the states but they came to be resolved not 'as between two governments, but between two wings of the same party.' Added to this was the charismatic personality of Nehru that overshawdowed the Chief Ministers. The party exercised command over the state governments through the

Working Committee popularly known as High Command and the Central Parliamentary Board. These two were very powerful institutional mechanisms during the early days and commanded considerable respect. The Working Committee was the highest executive authority of the Congress with powers to issue instructions and to superintend, direct and control all Pradesh Congress Committees. The Central Parliamentary Board was the child of the Working Committee. It was created to regulate and coordinate Parliamentary activities of the Congress legislature parties. The Working Committee used to set the norms for action by the Congress Governments at the state and the Parliamentary Board played the role of an instructor to the state legislative parties. It was an instrument of Central intervention. Added to this was the tremendous dominance of Nehru within the Congress. Nehru did away with the distinction between the party and the Government after 1950 he became the Government itself.

It has been said that Nehru's treatment of state party units and the state governments depended upon his equations with the persons concerned. Nehru as the first Prime Minister started the practice of making the office of the Governor a dumping ground of the defeated Congress politicians, retired civil servants, defecting opposition leaders. Rajendraprasad is reported to have disapproved the tendency and unsuccessfully tried to dissuade Nehru from doing it. Nehru did not allow the non-Congress government at the state level to work. The inconvenient ministry in (Jammu and Kashmir) was summarily dismissed to replace it by puppet regimes. The eastern border nationalities were denied the 'luxury' of the elected government, and were administered by the Indian army.

The Nehru Government dictated the policies and issued

directives, guidelines etc. to the state governments on all matters. They were also subjected to centralised planning. The Planning Commission emerged as a powerful organization engaging the status of a supercabinet. It may be noted that Nehru was the pioneer of the practice of increasing inequality among the states. This is illustrated by a study of non-plan, non-statutory but discretionary budgetary transfers made by the Centre to the states.

Nehru used the Governors and Rajpramuks in Travancore-Cochin, Madras and PEPSU respectively in 1952 to prevent the formation of non-Congress governments or to distress the non-Congress governments when it was formed (PEPSU). In 1957 the Congress combined the method of central intervention from above and direct action from below to overthrow the first non-Congress government in the country. Behind the Congress manaeuvres were the desparate moves of the insecure bourgioisie in the face of mounting crisis of the capitalist development. The development of capitalism necessitates, as one of its conditions, the formation of larger markets for commodity production. This necessity plus the requirement of big capital demand growing centralization.

It has been suggested by scholars like Amal Ray that India's federal system functioned more or less smoothly during the early days of Nehru. He feels that part of the explanation lies in "the persistence of earlier 'consensus' system.[4] He further observes that a relatively homogeneous elite both at the national and regional levels further facilitated the process. It was the urban middle class elite which provided main political support to the operation of India's federal system. In a recent article he has referred to the tradition of elite accommodation and organisational culture of informal federalism within one party dominance as providing a conducive atmosphere for the functioning of the federal policy."[5]

During the days of Nehru there was no great conflict between the captains of industry who envisaged a dominant role of the state in the modernisation of the economy, and those of agriculture. The Pradesh Congress Committees largely represented the interest of the latter. But soon after the Green Revolution in the 60s the landed interests began to increase their strength. For example, in Uttar Pradesh they increased their representation from 38 per cent in 1952 to 42 per cent in 1962. In the national legislature the agricultural lobby also increased its percentage of membership from 21 per cent in the first Lok Sabha to 27 per cent in the third Lok Sabha.[6]

The Exit of Nehru and the Rise of State Assertiveness

Nehru's death in 1964 signalled the bginning of an era of state assertiveness in Indian politics. The states played a very vital role in the succession and demonstrated that they would no longer be the 'yes persons' of the Central Government. His successor Lal Bahadur Sastri sought to evolve a new political culture of running the government through consultation and compromise. But he died before anything took concrete shape.

On the eve of the 1967 general elections the Indian state had become very centralized. The public sector in the Indian economy at the national level began to take shape and was quite dominant in some sectors. The 1967 general elections brought an end to the phase of one party dominance. The Congress Party lost its dominance in 8 states where the governments were formed by the regional parties with strong regional support base and largely representing the rural rich. The DMK Government in Tamil Nadu took the question of inter governmental relations to the political plane by constituting the Rajamannar Committee. It was the first of its kind in the country and the report was the first detailed systematic study of the different facets of the problem of centre-state relations.

The 1967 general elections which threw the Congress Party out of power in many states brought back the Congress Party in power at the Centre with a reduced majority. The Congress Party at the centre was engaged in regaining its hold over the electrorate. It took up the programme of containing growing rural unrest and destabilizing the opposition led governments at the state level. The centralization of powers was given a greater push by raising the slogan of national integrity, unity and security.

Political instability was followed by economic crisis. Javeed Alam observes that in such a situation the inability of the government to dole out concessions to the dominant landed interests uniformly all over leads to discrimination and consequent dissatisfaction. This is likely to lead to conflict of interests within the same ruling class across the regions. Likewise, though in a different way, the non-big bourgeoisie may be objectively hampered by the operation of the market laws. Such a condition along with the crystallized feelings of linguistic cultural oppression seems to have provided the material basis far non-big bourgeoisie in certain areas with a district population composition like Tamil Nadu to strike a balance with the landlords there.[7] Under these circumstances the locally placed ruling class groups seek greater powers for themselves through regional parties in power.

The Emergence of Mrs. Gandhi

The Congress Party adopted the strategy of split for refurbishing its image before the eyes of the people. The 1971 general elections resulted in a clean sweep of the ruling Congress Party. States were reduced to the subservient units of the centre. It was a period of growing centralization of party functioning. It was a period which witnessed the imposition of party nominees as chief ministers in states ruled by the Congress. It was a period which initiated the process of stalling the democratic functioning of the party by imposing nominated persons as office bearers at the pradesh committe (P.C.C.) levels. Mrs. Gandhi in her desire to strengthen the organization crushed the voices of dissent in the party and sought to built up an organization packed by yes-men and women : Indira is India became the slogan. Personal compulsions began to condition her political conduct. She accommodated the DMK government at Tamil Nadu and C.P.I.—led coalition in Kerala as long as it was necessary to subserve her political interests. She knocked off the DMK government the moment the DMK support became unnecessary to her political career. She unleased a trend of personalizing power structure. H. S. Verma comments, "The formal structure of the party got completely devalued and potitical non-entities acquired control of levers of power. The informal infrastructure of the party got too much narrowed down just below the top that ultimately below Indira Gandhi only four men exercised political power."

The Governors became personal nominees of Mrs. Indira Gandhi after 1969, and they were assigned the duty of protecting the interests of the centre. It was in many eases the job of the Governor to see that the state legislature was kept in 'animated suspension' or 'dissolved', as commanded by New Deihi. She overrode the established method of selecting chief minister on the basis of support in state assemblies. It was phase of 'demise of mediated politics and the rise of plebiscitary politics'. The imposition of Emergency completed the process by reducing the states to the 'vasals of of the centre'. The states were reduced 'to the status of thh subordinate departments of the centre under the aegis of the Central Home Ministry." During the dark days of Emergency the state ministries or legislatures were put under a "perpetual threat of being removed by hook or by crook, if they did not toe the line of the centre"[8] During the Emergency days the Constitution (Forty Second Amendment) Act, 1976 was introduced to further augment the authority of the centre. Education was transferred from the state list to the central list. The Central Government was authorised to deploy unilaterally its forces like Central Reserve Police Force, Border Security Force in any part of the country.

The Growth of the Big Bourgeoisie and Rich Peasantry

The rise of Mrs. Grandhi was accompanied by the growing enrichment of the big bourgeoisie and rich peasantry. In the case of top 20 industrial houses the growth was remarkable : the value of assets was recorded in 1969 increased by 25.9 per cent, 38.9%, 61.3% and 83.7% in 1972, 1973, 1974 and 1975 respectively.[9] The Green Revolution augmented the income of the big farmers. The purchasing power of the rural rich also increased because of rising procurement prices, growing credit facilities and subsidies. The shift of terms of trade in favour of agriculture added to this process even further.[10]

It is interesting to note, as Satyamurthi observes, that the influence of the Congress among the rich and middle peasantly began to be eroded during the phase of Emergency. He has identified the following factors for this change in Congress party's support base.

(1) The centre came under the increasing pressure from the industrial capital to release some of the surplus derived from the agriculture. It was suggested that following the achievement of self sufficiency in food balance between industrial and agricultural capital has to be reconstituted by a suitable change of government policy at the state level. Pressures were mounted to reduce the quantum of grants for agricultural development, to bring down the procurement prices of agricultural commodities and to introduce a measure of agricultural taxation.

(2) The rural poor bore the brunt of repression by the land owing community. Over a period of time they also felt disenchanted with the Congress and other non-left regional parties which came to power in 1967.[11]

The Janata Interlude

The political environment of India's federalism underwent an apparently structural change following the 1977 general elections. National political power was transferred from the hands of the Congress to those of a loose-knit Janata coalition representing a great variety of ruling interests. The 1967 general elections marked the beginning of transformation of the Indian political system from a dominant one party system to a multi-party system. In the absence of a viable compromise formula their different social bases and mass support forced them, as Javeed Alam observes, "to horse trade within the Janata to so tilt the policies that their mass support could be sustained...... The absence of internal cohesion as well as intra-party consensus on vital issues or on modalities on handling crisis situation made it difficult for it to impose its will or to effectively protect or guide the ruling classes".[12] The federal system was made open to bargaining because of the rise of the Janata Party in power at the centre. The Janata Government "formulated and tried to implement and institutionalize a neo-gandhian alternative to the centralized state and industrially oriented growth strategy associated with the Congress rule".[13] But there was some problem at the party level. The Janata Party was a 'motley crowd of disparate elements' assembled together because of historical compulsions. The party failed to develop sound ideological position. The composition of the pradesh committees displayed a lack of ideological homogeneity and cohesion.

The party did not make any 'breakthrough' in the field of political processes operating in the sphere of inter-governmental relationships. The state units were not allowed a free play. It followed the tradition of giving central directives to the states. For example, the Madhya Pradesh Government was directed to drop its mini—MISA and cooperative nomination ordinances although it was within the powers of the State Government. The Congress Ministry in Kerala was not given the opportunity of demonstrating its majority on the floor of the assembly. No positive steps could be taken towards alteration of the existing intergovernmental arrangement in the constitutional—legal sense. It, however, gave considerable political elbow room to states where non-congress parties were voted to power. For example, the Left Front Government in West Bengal could strike relatively independent path without the fear of being harrassed or toppled. During the short lived Janata Party rule the regional governments had enjoyed some degree of operational autonomy.

The Congress (I)'s Come Back

The Janata government which broke down under the pressure of mounting organisational crisis was soon replaced by the Congress (I) Party in 1980. The re-appearance of the Congress Party in the governmental scene was marked by two important shifts in Indian politics. In the first place, the rural rich emerged as a formidable national force capable of claiming a share in the national power cake. Charan Singh as the Prime Minister of the caretaker government championed the cause of the rich peasanty, in favour of shift in the terms of trade between industry and commerce. Secondly, the Janata Government strengthened the capitalist development in India. It took the initiative to open up the manufacturing industry to powerful thrusts of foreign and multinational capital.

It should be mentioned that the Indian political system was then passing through a phase of serious strains and stresses. Mrs. Gandhi began to deal with the crisis by adopting a centralized and authoritarian model of decision making. Mrs. Gandhi's attack on the federal structure began by dismissing a number of Janata governments. When the Congress (I) came back to power in 1980 a few states still had very stable Non-Congress Governments. The federal question was, however, kept alive by the Left Front Government in West Bengal. Within the Congress a sort of centre-state tension began to grow. The accent of the central leadership on the loyalty of the chief ministers towards itself brought about dissensions within the congress in most states.

In the early 80s number of agitations in Punjab and Assam added a new political dimension to the federal system. The Central Government adopted a centrist attitude. It sought to divide these movements, which became unsuccessful. The centre now began to act with a heavy hand. In Assam elections were imposed without adequate safeguards. In Punjab as the elections were fast approaching, the centre struck with a massive army operation.

The Growing Demand for Overhauling Center-State Relationships

A very significant feature in the field of centre-state relations in 1980s is the coming together of the opposition parties for retexturing the federal polity around the autonomy principle. This was given a concrete shape in the enclaves held at Hyderabad, Calcutta and Srinagar. "Their cooperative endeavour not only placed them in a position to demand share in decision making on major national issues but also brought about much needed credibility for federal politics".[14]

The growing cooperation among the oppossion parties for launching a movement to demand restructuring of centre-state relations led to a belligerent reaction on the part of the Central Government as it restricted its freedom to manoeuvre. The Congress party was also getting alarmed as it was likely to cast a shadow on the electoral prospect of the party. The party raised the bogey of the rise of 'anti-national' forces in the country as the Punjab situation was assuming on alarming turn. In the name of securing and consolidating the unity and integrity of the country the Central Government began to behave in an openly partisan manner in its dealing with the states. It has been said, "it was a re-run of the post-67 situation except that the slogan for 'unitarism' was more blatant".[15] The centre resorted to a well-known method called toppling operation. Attempts were made to dismiss, if necessary, by engineering defection, the 'recalcitrant' state governments. The federal pulls were, however, very strong. In the wake of the ever-growing demand for re-examination of the existing arrangement of inter-governmental relations Mrs. Gandhi's government was compelled to constitute a committee under the Chairmanship of Justice Sarkaria to probe into the intricate labyrinth of centre-state relations. A manifest tendency in post 1980 elections was greater centralization of resources. Attempt was also made to transfer, to the centre the only elastic source of state's revenue namely, sales tax. Another characteristic feature was the augmentation of the repressive power of the state through the enactment of the National Security Bill 1980 which sought to bring back preventive detention and the enactment of the Disturbed Area (Special Courts) Amendment Bill, 1981 to bring it under the fold of the concurrent list. It amounted to the interference by the centre in the internal affairs of the state government and encroachment on the jurisdiction of the state as law and order was a state subject. This Act empowered the centre to declare an area disturbed and set up special courts for speedy trial of offences committed in disturbed areas. Satyamurthi observes. "In an epoch demanding power sharing between competing interests of the ruling class, the autonomous political behaviour of Mrs. Gandhi resulted in petrification of the centre's resources for compromise and consensus."[16]

Mrs. Gandhi who was assassinated, was succeeded by her son Rajiv Gandhi. Weiner says, "Rajiv Gandhi assumed the office of the Prime Minister at a time when the capacity of the Indian state to perform three tasks had seriously eroded : to maintain law and order in a sharply divided society ; to play a positive role in facilitating economic growth in an economy with a high saving rate, skilled managerial and technical personnel and promising entrepreneurial talent and to cope with an uncertain international security environment."[17] Rajiv Gandhi as the leader of the Congress and the Prime Minister of India promised a new reconciliatory and cooperative political order. He promised to take a fresh look at the old problems. This approach was signalled by his unexpected decision in October 1986 to drop Arun Nehru from his cabinet. It helped reducing antagonism between the centre and the states to some extent. Toward the end of the year he could win over two of the most effective leaders in the opposition. In Maharashtra, Sharad Pawar the leader of the Congress (S) agreed to merge his party with the Congress (I). He relinquished President's rule over Jammu and Kashmir and entered into an agreement with Dr. Farook Abdullah to head a caretaker government of the National Conference and Congress (I). Clearly, these were political moves designed to consolidate the strength of the Congress (I).

He gave a great push to India's capitalist development by inviting the multinationals and liberalizing trade policies. The monopoly houses' assets went on increasing. Politically he was placed in a difficult position. His party began to loose political dominance in many states. Temperamentally, he was intolerant of dissent and wanted to have personal dominance in the party. In 1984 he took active part in toppling the State Governments in Sikkim, Addhra Pradesh and Kashmir. He did not hesitate to brand the entire opposition as 'liar' in the floor of the house. As his party faced more and more electoral reverses in the assembly elections, and as his government became more and more involved in questionable defence deals like Bofors he fell back on his mother's style of functioning. His threat that if any state government took 'anti national' stance he would dismiss it regardless of its majority smacks of his authoritarian style of functioning. The 59th Constitution Amendment Bill which was pushed through was the culmination of the process. He did not allow a single chief minister of the party to be freely elected by the party at the legislative assembly. Sengupta comments : "He demands conformity in a very plural political system, and allows himself the delusion that he has the power to dismiss the irksome political plurality."[18] The Rajiv Gandhi government during the later years of its tenure could not talk to the states through the political channels. The bureaucratic channels were utilized for initiating dialogue with the states. This was a new trend in centre-state relationships.

Rajiv Gandhi attempted a concerted onslaught on our federal system in the name of responsive administration and decentralization. He had convened the conferences of the district collectors and addressed them, bypassing the state governments. He wrote letters directly to the pradhans of the village panchayat. The 64th Amendment Bill introduced by the Prime Minister in the Lok Sabha is an attempt to centralize power in the name of giving constitutional sanction to panchayats. The bill enables the centre to enact legislation concerning panchayats when such a thing should be left to the state governments, it provides access for the centre to the panchayats by means of direct financing of panchayats.

It was reinforced by the setting up of the National Informatics Centre (NIC) at Delhi for collection of data at the block level. An officer of the centre will be placed in every district to collect and computerize information at the district level and transmit it to the NIC. The information so gathered will be utilized for the preparation of the model district plans.

The floating of the concept of the centrally sponsored schemes is meant for reducing initiative of the state governments. It was decided in the National Development Council's meeting in 1970 that the value of centrally sponsored schemes would be limited to 1/6 or 1/7 of the quantum of assistance for state plans, and they should be in the nature the project's survey and research. While such schemes amounted to Rs. 77 crores out of a total of Rs. 497 crores in 1969-70 or 15.4 percent in 1977-78 they amounted to 53 percent.[19] Rajiv Gandhi government started new ones namely Jawahar Rojgar Yogna in which funds were sent direct to the district magistrates or Chief Secretaries, Zilla parishads.

Amal Ray has described the recent intensification of centre-state confrontation as 'the second generation strains'. He has tried to explain this phenomenon with reference to the change in the composition on the political elite. Rural elites' dominance in the legislature has been on the rise. There has been a full of representation of the professionals such as lawyers in the legislature from 35.6% to 22.2% in the 8th Lok Sabha elections. But the agriculturists have registered an increase from 22.5% to 38.3%[20]. The rich agriculturists belong to dominant social caste and advocate state autonomy as agriculture is state subject.

The Rajiv Gandhi government suffered a big electrol setback in the nineth Parliamentary elections held in 1989. The National Front is now in power. It is a minority government with a majority support—supported by the Bharatiya Janta Party and the left parties from outside. It is committed to reverse the trend toward centralization in Indian politics, to restore the democratic institutions in the country and to revitalize the political links between the centre and the states. It has started setting a commendable trend in centre-state relationship by consulting the states in matter of appointment of the governors. It is committed to utilize and develop mechanisms for centre-state consultation. It is, however, too early to make any definite statement about the shape of things to come in the field of centre-state relationship in India in view of a new kind of political configuration at the centre.

REFERENCES

1. K.C. Wheare, *Federal Government*, Fourth Edition, Oxford, 1963, p. 36.
2. Jawaharlal Nehru's Speech in the Constituent Assembly, July 5, 1947.
3. E.M.S. Namboodripad 'National Political Background of Indian Federalism' in K. Mathew Kurien and P.N. Varugheese (ed.) *Centre-State Relations*, Macmillan, Delhi, 1981.
4. Amal Ray, 'From Consensus to Confrontation : Federal Politics in India', *Economic and Political Weekly*, (EPW) October 2, 1982, p. 1620.
5. Amal Ray. 'The Sarkaria Commission's Perspective' *EPW*, May 28, 1988.
6. Stanley Kochanek, *The Congress Party of India*, Princeton University Press, Princeton, 1968, p. 382.
7. Javeed Alam, 'Class Political and National Dimensions of State Autonomy Movements in India', *Social Scientist*, August, 1982, p. 19.
8. S.K. Goyal, *Monopoly Capital and Public Policy*, Allied, New Delhi, 1979, pp. 53-58.

9. *The West Bengal Government Document on Centre-State Relations*, December 1, 1977.

10. Ranjit Shau, 'Indian Political Economy—1966-77, Marriage of Wheat and Whisky', *EPW* April 9, 1977.

11. T.V. Satyamurthi, 'Impact of Centre-State Relations on Indian Politics : An Interpretative Reckoning', *EPW*, September 23, 1989, p. 2137.

12. Javeed Alam, *op. cit.*, p. 21.

13. L.I. Rudolph and S.H. Rudolph, *In Pursuit of Lakshmi : The Political Economy of the Indian State*, Orient Longman, 1987, New Delhi, p. 163.

14. Nirmal Mukerji and Asis Banerjee, *Democracy. Federalism and the Future of India's Unity*, Uppal Publishing House, New Delhi, 1987, p. 21.

15. *Ibid.*, p. 22.

16. T.V. Satyamurthi, *op. cit.*, p. 2140.

17. Myron Weiner, 'Rajiv Gandhi : A Mid Term Appraisal' in *India Briefing*, 1987, p. 7.

18. B Sengupta, 'Bonaparte in the Making' *EPW*, January 2, 1989, p 11.

19 *Economic and Political Weekly*, July 1, 1989, p. 1435.

20. Amal Ray, 'The Sarkaria Commission Perspective', *op. cit.*

CHAPTER 4

Secularism in India : A False Promise

The term 'secular' is drived from the Latin word *seculum*, which means an age, an indefinite period of time, or the present age. The dictionary defines 'secularism' as the doctrine that morality should be based solely on regard to the wellbeing of manking in the present life, to the exclusion of all considerations drawn from belief in God or in a future state. In the West the secular state has evolved out of different kinds of historical situation. For example, in France, it emerged from centuries of struggle between the church and the state. In USA, the secular state is continuing to evolve on a basis of mutual good feeling between the church and the state.[1] Secularism as it has developed in the West, therefore, denotes, "the belief that the state, morals and education should be independent of religion."[2] It originated as a result of social wrongs preponderant in social practices, and as a "reaction to the selfishness of the wealthy, and the influential classes, the unreasoning opposition to political and religious freedom. . . ."[3]

Rise of Secularism in the West

Broadly speaking, secularism in the West was the result of the rise of capitalism, Renaissance and Reformation movements, development of science and technology and the emergence of bourgeois liberal democracy in the 19th century. The secular reaction in Europe produced a theory of the hegemonic state presiding over the civil society as the public authority. In the Christian tradition the autonomy of the sphere of 'Caesar' and that of God had been recognized. In the church-state controversy in the West the state came out victorious. Historically the seeds of secularism were sown in the early medieval controversy between the church and the state. Marsiglio of Podua deleniated two components of the secular state. The rights of citizens are independent of the faith they profess, and no man may be punished for his religion. The idea of church-state separatism is the last consequence of the principle of religion, liberty and of the neutrality of the state in religious matters.

The term 'secular' owes its origin and in large measure, its existence to the life and labour of George Jacob Holyake, who started a materialistic and nationalistic movement in England. He defines secularism as a 'system of ethical principles', and its aim is to substitute the piety of usefulness for the usefulness of piety. The essential principle of secularism is to seek human improvement by material means.

There may be four elementary positions in the relationship between the state and religion. At the one end we may conceive of completely antagonistic relationship namely, of a state, that is completely against religion. At the other end of the spectrum one can think of a state that is religious in the sense of adhering to a particular religion. In between there are two positions where the state purports either to be indifferent or neutral to religion or professes equal respect to all religions. The general understanding of secularism oscillates between the two middle positions, that is, a state neutral to religion, or alternatively, a state that treats all religions with equal respect.

Secularism : Indian Variety

There may be two possible models of secularism. In one model as in the West, there is complete separation between the religion and the state. This is non interventionist model. In another model the state is equidistant from all religions. India opts for the second—the non-discriminatory model. Indian secularism is based on the tolerance of faith—*sarba dharma samabhava*. Balraj Puri is of the opinion that the eurocentric concept of secularism is not entirely relevant to our situation. He argues that far most of the European Countries are not only uni-religious with a theocratic past, but also now have Christian political parties. India is not only multi-religious but also has never been theocratic. In ancient India *raja* and *rishi* represented two distinct traditions who were neither antoganistic nor usurped each other's domain. During the days of the Muslim rule the *badsha* and *ulama* had autonomous roles. Unlike in the West religion and polities was neither mixed nor divorced in India. D.E. Smith says that India has followed the American experience towards religion as such. Dr. Radhakrishnan writes, "When India is said to be a secular state it does not mean that we reject reality of an unseen spirit or the relevance of religion to life or that we exalt irreligion. . . . The religious impartiality of the Indian state is not to be confused with secularism or atheism.[5] Secularism is here defined in accordance with the ancient religious traditions of India. M.V. Kamath spelled it out as "neither a Godless state nor an irreligious nor an antireligious state".[6] Dr. Ambedkar said, "secular state really means what the Constitution is intended to mean."[7] Pt. Nehru held that secularism means "equal respect for all faiths and equal opportunities for all, irrespective of the faith they profess."[8]

The document that was adopted in 1950 nowhere explicity stated the term 'secular' except in Article 25 (2)(c). The provision reads as follows : "Nothing in this Article shall affect the operation of any existing law so as to prevent the state from making any law (a) regulating or restraining any economic financial, political or other secular activity which may be associated with religious practices". In fact, K.T. Shah moved an amendment to use the word 'secular', but it was rejected. It was only after a lapse of a quarter of a century (1976) that the word secular was inserted in the preamble. It was a time when the ruling party was gradually losing its Muslim support base following the imposition of Emergency. Mrs. Gandhi had initiated the move to incorporate the word 'secular' to win Muslim confidence by re-emphasising the 'secular' character of the state. Denying the proposition that secularism had strong roots in India's past, Sinha observes that a tradition bound, caste ridden and authoritarian society, unwilling to make a breach with the past, does not provide a nourishing soil for secularism to strike roots. In fact, in the pre-British days, the social basis of the state was the 'village community' with the ancient form of civilization and their hereditary means of subsistence. Religion helped to provide stability to the social structure of the village community—an ideology of the precapitalist social formations.

Secularism and the Nationalist Movement

The British colonial rulers made a compromise deal by retaining landlords' rule in Indian villages. They viewed Indians in terms of their religion and provided separate electorate to widen the gap between communities. In the second half of the 19th century the steady growth of the industries helped the Indian bourgeoisie to become strong politically and economically. In India the bourgeoisie had no interest in the development of rationalism. The British rulers' attempt to homogenize the country by breaking up the native communities uprooting of the native industry caused a sense of insecurity in the minds of the people. They fell back on religion to regain self-confidence. The liberal and extremist traditions of modern India bore the marks of religion. Throughout the nineteenth century the liberal and the non-liberal leaders perceived religion in terms of politics and politics in terms of religion. The extremists made political use of religion. Hindu symbols were employed to bring the people into the movement. Religious festivals were used for political propagation.

Gandhijis' appearence on the Indian political scene added a new dimension to the religion-politics syndrome. He used religion for mobilizing the masses. But he sought to evolve a strategy which is determined to avoid communal confrontation. This lead him to support secularism, although he did not make politics subservient to religion. The passion to make India secular was largely that of Nehru. In order to counter the unhealthy cleavage that had crept into Hindu-Muslim relations, following the collapse of the Khilafat movement, Nehru had taken a pre-emptive step in the 1931 Karachi Resolution of the Congress. The Resolution on Fundamental Rights Causes taken there became the cornerstone of the secularism in our Constitution. Thus the tragedy of the Indian national movement was that from the begining an overt and covert use of religion and religious slogans was made for political purposes. Following the legacy of Tilak and Aurobindo Ghosh Gandhiji used Hindu terminology like *Ramrajya*, *Kirtan* during prayer meetings and supported certain movements like *Goraksha*. Gandhiji combined in him two persons—Gandhi the politician and Gandhi the apostle of Hinduism. Nehru in his *Autobiography* bemoans the failure of the Congress leadership to cultivate secular values and scientific temper. The circumstances under which India became independent was most uncongenial for setting up a secular state. India did not succumb to the pressures of the Hindu communal forces.

Secularism in the Indian Constitution

The Indian Constitution guarantees equality of all citizens, irrespective of their religion, race, caste, sex, place of birth or any of them. It seeks to protect the cultures and languages of the religious and linguistic minorities. Article 26 offers any religious minority the right : (a) to establish and maintain institutions for religious and charitable purposes, (b) to manage its affairs in matters of religion, (c) to own and acquire immovable property, and (d) to administer such property in accordance with law. This notion of equality is co-extensive with the principle of protective discrimination. Aricle 16 (4) suggests that "nothing in this Article shall prevent the state from making any provision for the reservation of the appointments or posts in favour of the backward class of citizens which in the opinion of the state, is not adequately represented in the services under the state". In fact, there is a provision for reservation of seats in the various fields of administration and in professional and educational institutions for the Scheduled Castes and Tribes. There is, thus, no state religion, nor does a religion get patronage from the state. The public funds of the state cannot be used for the promotion of interests of any religious group. Thus the provisions of the Indian Constitution relating to secularism fall into four broad categories.

1. There are some provisions which prohibit the state from making distinctions between citizens ;
2. There are some provisions which guarantee freedoms of religion and religious institutions ;
3. Some provisions require the state to make special efforts for protecting the backward classes ; and
4. Some other provisions require the state to take special measures for the upliftment of the weaker sections to develop a uniform civil code.

Luthera argues that the Constitution of India does not establish a secular state. It establishes a state which is close to what he calls 'jurisdictional state', and is far away from a secular state. Luthera says that some of the provisions of India's Constitution do not forbid discrimination by the state on grounds of religion. He says, "The Constitution does not set up a 'wall' or partition between them (church and the state)". He argues "the power of the state to embark upon social reform legislation does not stop at the non-religious sphere but extends even to religious sphere. The state can amend and reform religious doctrine, dogma and laws...... The state can enact communal legislation applicable differently to different religious communities. It can make religion a ground for discrimination against or classification of citizens." On the other hand there are scholars like Mark Galanter for whom the Constitution is 'openly and determinedly secular'[9]. But there is no strict separation of religion from public life. Secularism in India means, theoretically speaking, four things : (i) the rejection of a quasi-theocratic state like that in Pakistan, (ii) the affirmation of non-religion based democracy ; (iii) the proclamation that religion is of private or group concern and (iv) the assertion of the unity and fraternity of the people of India and inalienable equality of all citizens of the republic, irrespective of their caste and creed

Hindrances to the Growth of Secularism in India

Secularism to be meaningful entails the supremacy of the democratic state—the supremacy of its laws and administration over the existing pre-democratic social formation marked by loyalties to tribe, caste, religion, language etc. Raseeduddin says "secularism in one dimension is 'rationalism' and in another, routinization of bureaucracy as the main instrument of organizing a civic society. Secular character of the state is manifested through the respectful indifference to religions and keeping vigilant distance from the politics of religious communalism."[10]

Secularisation of polity does not take place by the use of the secular rehtorics. It requires a basic change in the institutional framework of economy and polity of the country. In our country the working class could not establish its hegemony over the national liberation movement. It is an integral part of the social set up that vast sections of the people are under the sway of the backward ideologies. The ruling classes utilize them for reactionary purposes. Referring to this aspect of post colonial third world societies the Soviet scholars observe "None of the religions practised in the East-Islam, Buddhism and above all, Hinduism—has undergone radical bourgeois reformation. It means that in the new historical situation... traditional precapitalist, communalist religious consciousness comes out as a natural reaction of the small proprietor strata to new phenomena. It should be borne in mind that in a number of Afro-Asian countries a purely secular ideology... ordinarily cannot, with the speed required by history, replace the traditional communalist, clan, caste, estate, tribal, semi-feudal religious fanatic ideology as the day to-day ideology of the tens of millions of small owners...Hence their adherence to tribal, caste and religio-ethical standards."[11] This point has also been strongly made by Namboodripad. To quote "As a matter of of fact, the very growth of capitalism, the rise of the bourgeois and proletarian classes, was and is coloured by the persistence of the old Varna society. Neither of the two major classes of the emerging capatilist society, the bourgeoisic and the proletariat, could shake of the pre-capitalist modes of thinking and culture".[12] After Independence India adopted the capitalist path of development which brought with it attendant evils like economic inequality, uneven development, etc. Again, capitalism in India is different from capitalism in the West. The colonial rule in India imposed capitalism in this country on the existing feudal system as a result of which Indian capitalism began to develop along with feudalism which in the West was destroyed to pave the road for capitalism. Thus the primordial loyalties of the pre-capitalist society continued to operate despite the growth of the capitalism. Again capitalism in India is very weak compared to that in the West. Capitalism in the West was fed by the exploitation of the colonial hinterland. As the third world countries do not have colonies, it would not develop as its counterpart did in the west. Thus capitalism in India is co-existing with feudalism because big bourgeois-led Congress Government compromised with landlordism to create new state power. It means compromise with all those elements of superstructure which propped up the old feudal landlordism. It is significant to note that the communal violence in India today is widespread in 'cow belt' where fedualism is quite strong.

The imperialist domination was a great hindrance to the growth of the Indian capitalist class. The penetration, control and eventual establishment of the hegemony over the economy of the country by a metropolitan bourgeosie was instrumental in frustrating the development of an indigeneous capitalist class. It is evident from experiences of other colonial countries that "class structures are shaped in directions which destroy the very conditions of self sustaining capitalist development and growth. Such are historical circumstances that may not necessarily move the national bourgeoisie to consistent anti-feudal and anti-imperalist positions in the spheres of society, economy and polity. The passage to independence, its form and content, may then lack the motive force for an adequate social transformation. ...Thus the entire lineage of progress from feudalism to capatalism, became a caricature of itself."[13] Thus in a given situation the capitalist class could not become the bearer of modern ideology like secularism.

The process of secularisation of Indian polity received further jolt following the growth of unevenness in India's economic development which is an offshoot of capitalism. Ranjit Sau's study of Indian capitalism suggests that the rate of profit is much higher in the bigger companies than that of the smaller ones. The increasing gulf between the two types of companies means that "the fate of the petty capitalists is tied up with that of the small companies...on balance, it can therefore be said that the prospects for graduation of petty capitalsits in India into the ranks of the capitalists are somewhat dim.[14] The transition of the landlords and capitalist farmers into the class of industrial capitalists seems also impossible. The administered prices, particularly those related to steel, cement, and telescopic railway freight in the context of coal and similar other policies were oriented to aid and support the monopoly sector in total disregard of the interest of the under-developed regions.[15]

In the field of agriculture the same picture is noticeable. The process of land reforms came to a halt, after the end of fifties except in some states ruled by the leftists. The infrastructural prop to agriculture in terms of massive and widespread public investment in water management and power which have provided technological support to bourgeoisie development in rural India, was deliberately neglected. The whole approach to agricultural development was related to encouraging production in selected pockets. The peasantry in India could not become the bearer of secularism, although they made significant contribution to the nationalist movement. In fact, the nationalist movement and peasant movement dıd not grow into an anti-colonial anti-feudal revolution.

The four decades of experience of our mixed economy demonstrate that in effect it has led to the growth of state capitalism. Monopoly capital has flourished and privileged sections have prospered. Its effect has been commercialization and marketization of rural economy as a resultof which 'rural ethos' and social relations have undergone marked changes. Traditional social inequality as represented through caste is being replaced by sharp economic inequality. The benefits of public policies have gone into the pockets of a few. The nationalised institutions serve the interests of the big industrial bourgeoisie. The public financial institutions came in support of the big industrial houses in a big way.[16] The public sector in the framework of the capitalist mode of production has not promoted socialism (if it can ever do so) but provided at state cost the infrastructure of power, energy, coal, iron steel etc., that facilitated the growth of the sprawling capitalist system in India. Rasheeduddin says "At best the public sector represents the segment of state capitalism, more as a cooperative rather than as competitive element in the given economic system, creating a contradictory problem of 'growth and poverty' and not of growth eliminating poverty."[17] The recent thrust of the policies of poverty alleviation has proved to be counter productive and wasteful. The co-existence of poverty and prosperity is a basic feature of India's economy. India ranks according the reports of the World Bank, eighth in global count for overall industrial production : seventh in iron-ore, sixth in coal and manganese, fourth in grain, third in railways, and third also in the number of scientific and technical personnel. But the process of industrialization is still far behind the requisite level of development that could stabilize the basis of a self-reliant and self-generating economy. The ever increasing balance of trade deficit and a massive foreign debt around Rs. 97,000.00 crores are clear indications of our movement away from the path of self reliant growth. Inflation has become an integral part of the planned development since the mid 60s. It served the interests of the big bourgeoisie in many ways. For example it reduced the real income of the rentier and wage earner classes. It also resulted in reduced gains to small and medium level industrial activities because of their limited capacity of hold stocks either of raw materials, or of intermediate goods or of finished products. In the absence of overall development, the fedual ethos, though in some degrees, pervade the country. People enmeshed in feudal identities like caste, creed, communal, ethnic etc. keep away from the scientific outlook.[18]

In Europe during the Middle Ages, the church and the state had been inseparable for a considerable period. The segregation of the church from the state became possible through the constitution of civil society which organised the domains of production and reproduction of individuals. On the other hand, the state became the arena of collective action. The institutionalized character of the Christianity as the predominant religion in Europe facilitated the process of separation of religion from politics there. Besides, Hindu religion is different from the institutionalized character of the Christianity. Hindu religion is very old and India is a traditional society. The state in India has not been so powerful and dominant as to enter the far-flung villages. The states' presence is hardly felt there. The recent case of 'Sati' at a Rajasthan village and the resistance of the local population against the policemen showed how deep is the influence of religions on their social life. In India, secularism implies the co-existence and toleration of all religions. All religions are equal before the state. In such a situation the distinction between state and civil society gets blurred as the civil society remains unconstituted.

The European experience suggests that secularism can grow in an atmosphere where democracy permeates the social fabric and where democratic institutions are allowed to have a free play. Pt. Nehru had some respect for the democratic institutions like party, press, Parliament etc. Democracy became a casualty during the days of Mrs. Gandhi. Democratic procedures within the Congress were replaced by nominations from above, and the organisational culture of democratic decision-making based on negotiations and compromises was mercilessly crippled. Amal Ray writes, "A period of repression began in the sense of deliberately bringing about an authoritarian, executive-centred system of government and extracting mobilizational capacities through mass manipulation."[19] All these resulted in a conflictual political culture with low levels of legitimacy. The ruling party in India led by Mrs. Gandhi sought to deal with the 'legitimacy' crisis of the Indian state by making some tall promises like *garibi hatao* on the one hand, and by increasing the coercive authority of the state through the imposition of the Emergency, on the other. India's bourgeois democratic edifice crumbled into pieces following the imposition of Emergency. India witnessed an era of highly centralized politics. Voices of dessent were muffled. Rajiv Gandhi carried forward the tradition. In fact, a party which does care for internal democracy in its working cannot help grow democracy in the country. As the state began to fast loose its 'legitimacy' in the eyes of the public as a result of the growing crisis and as his party's image began to erode following the exposition of scandals the ruling Congress party became more centrist and the leadership more authoritarian. The Rajiv Gandhi Government adopted the method suggested by Mrs. Gandhi. It tried to stem the growing erosion of the state 'legitimacy' first by taking recourse to the coercive authority of the state as in the case of the 69th amendment and second, by talking of the revitalization of grassroots democracy, employment of a least one member in each family etc. Kothari suggests that "the Indian state in the 80s became increasingly centralized and exclusive. There had been increasing use of repression and terror against the poor and the weaker sections. State and society became the playgrounds for a whole lot of upstarts." He continues "what is seen is not the crisis of politics, but its death."

The ruling classes have resorted to a range of cultural policies in the name of practising secularism which have strengthened their hold on power rather than promoting secularism. Mohanty suggests that the policies of the Indian state which claims to be secular have been hegemonic in two respects. In the first place, they seek to promote the interest of the ruling parties by manipulating various religious groups. "When it has suited the Congress (I) it has given the appearance of protecting the interests of the minorities. On other occasions and in general, it has carefully maintained its Hindu base. Secondly, the development strategy in India has had a streamrolling effect ostensibly advancing universality and rationality, but actually disorienting cultural identity groups. In fact, the so-called secular development process has mainly served the hegemonic purposes of the state."[20]

The management of education and policies associated with it have by and large operated as a drag on promotion of scientific outlook and ethos. They dampen the development of the bourgeoisie culture. It has been witnessed that the big bourgeoisie invokes pre-capitalist culture, traditional values, religious overtones when it comes to defend its interests. It is interesting to mention here that Nehru himself was doubtful about the successful growth of secularism in India. He felt that a caste-ridden society was not properly secular.

It was since the days of Mrs. Gandhi that the communlization of polity came to the fore. In a secular democracy the ruling party's credentials have to be above suspicion. The disintegration of the Janata experiment led the Congress to woo Hindu voters, the phenomenon becoming explicit after the 1980 elections. Attention of the Indian state was shifted from the basic economic and political tasks to communal and ethnic issues. She lost Muslim support considerably during and after the Emergency and since 1980 she tried to rally the support of the Hindu middle class. She tried to exploit the Meenakshipuram conversions and lent subtle support to Viswa Hindu Parishad (VHP). In an effort to retain the Hindu support communalism was integrated into the functioning of the state.[21] It is however difficult to establish causal connection, but the fact remains that some of the most gruesome and long drawn communal riots between 1980-84 Moradabad (UP) 1980, Allahabad (UP) 1980, Godhara (Gujarat) 1980-81, Biharshariff (Bihar) 1981, Ahmedabad (Gujarat), 1982 Hyderabad (A.P.) 1983, Bhiwandi, Bombay (Maharashtra) 1984, to cite a few examples took place with the complicity of the police and administration in general. Mrs. Gandhi's credibility with the Hindus rose so high in this period that she was able to drive a wedge between Bhartiya Janata Party (BJP) and Rashtriya Swayam Sevak Sangha (RSS).

The whole strategy became explicit in 1983 when Mrs. Gandhi refused to allocate blame, though the Shiva Sena chief played an important role in fomenting communal violence in Bhiwandi. In the Jammu and Kashmir elections of 1983, she openly showed her ability to play the Hindu card and the performance was repeated in Delhi elections with the help of the RSS. Under her leadership the Congress became very close to RSS in Maharashtra. It is significant to note that the big bourgeoisie helped the process of encouraging Hindu communal sentiments of the people. A number of temples came up and the monopoly houses provided funds for this purpose. Congress-I's attempt to recoup its position in Punjab by patronizing the Sikh extremists let loose a storm of communal politics. After her death RSS openly supported the Congress in the 1984 general elections and this alliance continued upto the Assembly elections of 1985. This phase saw the rise of the Viswa Hindu Parishad (VHP) and other frontal Hindu organisations all over the country.

Rajiv Gandhi's 1984 elections campaign was based in part on Hindu backlash support : sympathy for a breaved son whose mother died martyr to a Hindu cause and a campaign appeal for national unity that spoke to Hindu nationalism. The rise of Mr. Rajiv Gandhi in Indian politics and the steady decline of his Mr. clean image as a result of his alleged involvement in scandals like Bofore and other military deals worsened the situation further. As the Rajiv Gandhi's Congress began to steadily lose its traditional support base the Congress party started wooing the communalists for getting both the Muslim and Hindu votes. In the Shah Banu case the Government played the Muslim Card in 1986 by passing Muslim Women's (Protection of Rights on Divorce) Bill, 1986. The law preserved the independence and integrity of Muslim personal law which the orthodox Muslims alleged the Supreme Court's judgement in the Shah Bano case (1985) had put at risk. The concept of uniform civil code suffered a jolt.

The ruling Congress party played the Hindu card very openly just on the even of the last general elections. The communal couldron has been boiling for sometime following the Babri Masjid—Ram Janmabhumi controversy. The ruling Congress party at Uttar Pradesh bypassed the Supreme Court order relating to the disputed land and allowed the religious bigots to lay the foundation stone of a new temple at Ayodhya (UP). The speed and confidence with which the VHP and its associated organizations went about their task showed that they had reached a secret understanding with the ruling party at Lucknow and Delhi. The Congress party had also played the Christian card in north-east Indian states like Mizoram in the Christian majority constituencies. Rudolph and Rudolph observe "the circumstances of the early and mid 80s have led to a gradual re-definition of the state's religious stance from a secularism that recognised individual citizens entitled to free practice of religion to a secularism that is obliged to recognize corporate religious groups clamouring for protection and advantage"[22] Clearly the political processes in post-Independence India were supposed to Nurture and strengthen the secular values, proceeded along different directions. Randhir Singh seems to be right when he suggests "the heightening of communalism today is simultaneously the product of soil, moral and political crisis in society and the reaction of the ruling classes to this crisis. With the older bases of their power and hegemony weakening, they are increasingly turning to communalism to win votes, fragment and divide the people and above all, secure their continued political and ideological dominance over them."[23]

Thus the state in independent India which was supposed to eradicate communalism to clear the deck for secularism has become the generator of anti-secular values by its sections (as in the case of the Shah Banu) or by its active collusion with the fundamentalist forces (as in the case of the laying foundation stone at Ayodhya.) Can a state the ruling party's statesmen of which seek the blessings of the Hindu saints before starting election campaigns, be secular ? Can the federal India one of whose chief ministers is allowed to do official work in the dress of a Hindu monk, be a secular one ? Can the ruling party which uses the state—owned electronic media to preach mythological Hindu glories and subsequently utilizes the image of the role actors for electoral campaigns, make India secular ? Rajni Kothari suggests that the development policy of the state has led to greater centralization and exclusion of larger and larger protection of people from the institutional fold of politics thus driving them into communal solidarities.[24] Thus politics of the ruling classes in a society with a massive feudal colonial inheritance, deep religions divisions undergoing its own historically specific form of capitalist development need to be examined to explain the state of secularism in India. The ruling classes in India have used secular ideals as a means of seeking legitimacy to the state which has failed to deliver the goods. It has deliberately ignored the social tasks associated with the development of a secular society[25]. It is too simplistic to attribute the decline of secularism to the mismatch between secularism as a Western credo and Indian culture, [6] or simply to the identity seeking aspirations of socially mobile groups as Rudolph and Rudolph have done. The roots have to be sought in the base and superstructure of Indian society and in the processes of their interaction, besides the historical backdrop of shifting imperial policies of accommodation and the nationalist struggle. In the Constituent Assembly, the conservatives considered Hinduism as a fundamental element in the field of politics, and envisaged a new India in terms of the glories of the ancient Hindu kingdoms and led opposition to the measures like the Hindu Code Bill.[27] The liberal rulers of Independent India 'renamed India as Bharat in tune with the old Hindu tradition, made efforts to evolve Hindi as an all India language with an emphasis on Sanskritisation, even to the extent of eliminating any trace of Muslim culture ; selected national symbols (Dharma Charka and others) ; and desired to resurrect certain cultural values of pre-Muslim past, popularized religious and superstition-ridden festivals (Ramlila and others) and other programmes ; organized Sadhu Samaj and thereby made use of the most orthodox and most consciously conservative section of the society as an agent of moral and social transformation and that too under people to introduce teaching of religion in educational institutions ; to inculcate school education with superstition, broadcast Bhajans and devotional songs in the early morning programme of the Radio generating helpless moods of depending on mystical power and propagated 'back to the Vedas and Gita' ; even Nehru advocated a basic approach to India's problems on Vedantic lines"[28].

Concluding Observations

It cannot however be, denied that the connection between religion and politics runs deep. The powerful ideas of German reformation, French enlightenment and British materialism have failed to relegate religion to the level of social and political insignificance. In the advanced capitalist countries where secularism has been accepted as an operative principle and the secularization process has been strengthened by the momentus achievements of science and technology, religion continues to influence the political processes. The ruling classes use religion to maintain *status quo* in the society. Marx writes, "religion is at the same time the expression of real distress and also the protest against real distress. Religion is the sigh of the oppressed creature, the heart of heartless world, just as it is the spirit of spiritless conditions. It is the opium of the people."

Hinduism is one of the oldest religions of the world. The state in India is yet to reach out to the people in the far flung villages who are steeped in the traditional ideas. Religion is very strong there, and conditions the life processes of the individual. The incident of Sati which took place in Rajasthan a few years back goes to show how religious prescriptions influence the life activities and mould the way of life of the individuals in villages. In fact, every religion has its profound influence on the people. The recent restlessness of the religious nationalities in the USSR tend to show that religion continues to influence the social actions of the individuals even after seven decades of socialist construction. "The fight for secularism", as Mohanty observes, "has to be oriented against the hegemony of the Indian state and ruling forces in Indian society. Politics of hegemonic secularism has failed in India. Democratic secularism may reassure the identity groups in the process of struggle for democratic transformation in India.[29] In West Bengal where the Left Front imbued with Marxist ideology has been in power for more than a decade the record of communal solidarity is very impressive. It shows the significance of ideology of the ruling parties in the promotion of secularism.

REFERENCES

1. D.E. Smith, *India as Secular State*, Princeton, New Jeresy, 1963, p. 21, for a World Historical Perspective, see, M. Bhattacharya, 'Secularism and Nation Building in India' in B. Chakraborty (ed.) *Secularism and Indian Polity*, Segment Book Distributors, New Delhi, 1990.

2. *Chamber's Twentieth Century Dictionary*, (Rinesed Edition), 1959, p. 1000.

3. Article on Secularism in *Encyclopedia of Religion and Ethics*.

4. Balraj Puri, 'Politics of Ethnic and Communal Identities', *Economic and Political Weekly*, April 7, 1990.

5. S. Radhakrishnan, *Recovery of Faith*, Quoted in V.P. Luthera, *The Concept of a Secular State and India*, OUP, 1964, p. 202.

6 M.V. Kamath, *Constituent Assembly Debates*, Vol II, Government of India, Delhi, 1951, pp 825-26.

7. B R Ambedkar, *Parliamentary Debates*, Part II, Vol II, Vol VIII, Government of India, Delhi, 1951, Column 2466.

8. R. Zakaria, (ed.) *Indian Unity : A Symposium on its Different Facets*, Popular Prakashan, Bombay, 1967, p. 26.

9. V.P. Luthera, *The Concept of the Secular State and India*, Oxford University Press, London, 1964.

10. Reseeduddin Khan, 'Secularisation Process in India : Problems and Prospect, in Iqbal Narain, (ed.) *Development, Policies and Social Theory* : Essays in Honour of Professor S.P. Verma, Sterling Publishers, Delhi, 1989, p. 143.

11. R. Ulyanovosky and U. Pavolv, "The Asian and African Countries : Specific Features of Development" *Social Sciences*, (Moscow) No. 4, 1980.

12. E.M S Namboodripad, 'The Indian National Question : Need for a Deeper Study' *Social Scientist*, Vol. 10, No. 12, 1982, p 68.

13. Asoke Sen, "Transition for Socialism to Capitalism' *Economic and Political Weekly* (EPW), Review of Political Economy, July, 1984, p. 58.

14. Ranjit Sau, 'The Development of Capitalism in India', *EPW*, July, 1984, p. 75, Prabhat Patnaik 'Imperialism and the Growth of Capitalism' in Blackburn, (ed.) *Explosions in a Sub-continent*, Penguin, 1975, p. 51-79.

15. Pradhan H. Prasad, *Lopsided Growth* Smeeksha Trust and OUP, 1989, pp. 2-3.

16. S K. Goyal, Organised Sector : Directions of Change IIPA, New Delhi, 1988, Nirmal Chandra, *The Retarded Economics*, Smeeksha Trust and Oxford, 1989, pp. 295-98.

17. Rasedduddin Khan, *op. cit*, pp.

18. Pradhan H. Prasad, *Lopsided Growth, op. cit.*, pp. 2-3, pp. 73-92.

19. Amal Ray, 'From a Constitutional to an Authoritarian System of Government : Interaction between Politics and Constitution in India' *Journal of Commonwealth and Comparative Politics*, p. 287.

20. Monoranjan Mohanty, Secularism : Hegemonic and Democratic, *EPW*, June 3, 1989.

21. Anjan Ghosh, 'Does the Indian State Speak of Hindus ?' *Times of India*, August 27, 1987.

22. Lloyd Rudolph and Susanne Rudolph, *In Pursuit of Lakshmi : The Political Economy of Indian State*, Orient Longman, 1987, p. 9.

23. Randhir Singh, 'Theorising Communalism : A Fragmentary Note on the Marxist Mode' *EPW*, July 23, 1988.

24. Rajni Kothari, 'Inclusion and Exclusion in Indian Politics' *EPW*, 1988.

25. Krishna Kuma, 'Secularism : Its Politics and Pedagogy', *EPW*, Nov. 4-11, 1989.

26. See J.N. Madan, Secularism in its Place, *The Journal of Asian Studies* November, 1987.

27. M Mohanty, *op. cit.*

28. Granville Austin, *The Indian Constitution : Cornerstone of a Nation*, Bombay, 1962, p. 284.

29. A.R. Desai, *Recent Trends in Indian Nationalism*, Bombay, 1960, pp 132-34.

CHAPTER 5

Reservation : A Policy in India

Reservation policy in India owes its origin to the days of the colonial rule. The Mandal Commission dated the origins of special treatment to the Grant in Aid Code of the Madras government in 1885, The Code provided special treatment for backward classes in the educational sphere. The Madras Government also pioneered the policy of reserving a share in the Government services to candidates from these classes. The colonial rulers introduced new land system. Land was made a freely marketable commodity. It was available for purchase by any caste. Thus the hereditary right in the produce of the client caste was discarded. The new relationship in the private ownership in land had considerably underestimated the patron-client relationship in India, and encouraged the growth of money economy. Land now began to be transferred from the cultivating classes to the class of the traders and moneylenders. This process which was noticeable in the western part of the country made it difficult on the part of the non Brahmin castes of Maharashtra to depend much on the traditional ccupation for their livelihood. This necessitated some of the members of these castes to go for modern education for the purpose of getting a job in the new British administrative system.

The Scheduled Castes, especially the Mahars of Maharashtra, could not remain isolated from this process of change, once the patron client jagmani network started breaking down, the Mahars with their unskilled traditional occupation naved from the villages to towns in search of employment. They were recruited in the army of Peshwas and latter on, in those of the East India Company.[1]

The Britishers made education compulsory for the Scheduled Caste (S.C.) recruits in order to strengthen their military base. It was necessary for the easy and proper operation of the military weapons. Significantly, educational facilities were extended to the general S.C. people in 1858. The initiation of the Mahars to the education process helped them to obtain requisite qualifications for serving the British administration, Bombay textile mills and the Indian railways.

Now the Non-Brahmin castes who had acquired the requisite qualification to enter the new occupation, and the Scheduled Castes of Maharashtra whose educational level was much lower to that of the non-Brahmin castes failed to compete with the Brahmins. The Brahmins came in contact with education much earlier. It was natural therefore that the Brahmins had at first availed themselves of the occupational opportunities available in Maharashtra.[2]

This was the background against the non-Brahmins and the

S.Cs., especially Mahars, under the leadership of Dr. Ambedkar demanded reservations in political and administrative field in Maharashtra. In Madras the non-Brahmins were also outnumbered by the Brahmins in political, economic and administrative fields. They also demanded reservation.[3]

The rise of capitalism and the growth of the commercial sector had affected the Muslims who were predominantly absorbed in the artisan industries. As the Muslims were pushed out from the leading position in the non-commercial traditional economy, they demanded special privileges to compansate for their inferiority to Hindu superiority.[4]

It was against this backdrop of demand for reservation that the colonial rulers formulated the policy of reservation using communal symbols like castes. This was necessary as they wanted to master the support of the different sections in India[5]. Clearly the problem of reservation in India arose in the context of a new class formation. It is not simply the outcome of the demand placed by the communal groups, but has to be understood against the background of the emerging capitalist structure in India.

Debates in the Constituent Assembly

It was Pt. Nehru who moved the Objectives Resolution of the Constituent Assembly promising to provide adequate safeguards for 'minorities, backward and tribal areas and depressed and other backward classes'. Reservations for the Harijans proposed soon to be listed as Scheduled Castes, received support from most of the members of the Constituent Assembly and some of the prominent members who spoke for reservations in fovour of the Harijans were V.I. Muniswami Pillai, H. J. Khandekar, Chandrika Ram.

A glance at the Constituent Assembly debates indicates that the perspective of the Constituent Assembly on reservations was shaped by two considerations. First, reservations were to be used in moderate measure, with a definite time frame in mind, and secondly, in such manner so as not to impinge too drastically on principles of merit and efficiency.

The purpose behind advocating a time limit that was supposedly open to being extended, was explained by many speakers. It was felt that limit would induce maximum effort and bring into operation the principle of effective review. It will offer, as H. N. Kunzru observed in the Constituent Assembly meeting, the legislature to see "how it has worked and how the state has discharged its duty towards the protected classes."

There was a consensus on reservation for the Scheduled Castes and Scheduled Tribes. It was argued that this was needed for fighting untouchability and to integrate these two groups within the larger society on a respectable basis. But the Assembly displayed a lack of unanimity when the issue of reservations for the backward classes came up for discussion. It was noted by many members that it was difficult to define the term 'backward' nor was it easy to find out suitable criteria for testing the backwardness of a community or a class. Dharam Prakash Phrasad the difficulty of defining the backward classes on a caste basis. The members also could not agree on whether reservations were the real cure for backwardness.

If there was any agreement on the issue of other backward classes in the Constituent Assembly, it was on the point that reservations meant for them should be in a moderate measure. In fact, the final drafting of the provisions concerning the backward classes had to reconcile different views on that subject. In the first place, many members felt that there should be equality of opportunity for all citizens and every individual should have his qualifications tested so as to determine whether he was fit for the post. Another dominant view in the house was that if this principle was to be put into practice there ought to be no reservations of any sort for any class or community. Then again a view shared by a fairly large number of members was that although it was theoretically sound to have the principle that there would be equality, provisions must also be made for the entry of certain communities which had not so far a proper 'look in', so to say, into the administration. While explaining his position regarding the final drafting of the provisions Dr. Ambedkar further maintained that the rule about the other backward classes reservations "would be a justiciable matter".

Reservations Provisions in the Constitution

There are two components in the reservation policy. One is what is called legislative reservations which under Article 334 of the Constitution have to be extended every 10 years. Another is job reservations mentioned in Article 16(4) 46 and 335. They do not have any time light. The first component thus relates to the polity, and second, to the economy. On September 12, 1947, the Government of India provided for 12.5 per cent reservation of vacancies for S.C. And on September 13, 1950 the Constitution provided for 5 per cent reservation for S. T. The percentage of reservation was revised on the basis of the 1961 census and in March 1970, the Government increased reservation to 15 per cent for the S.C. and 7½ per cent for S. T.

According to the latest report the Department of Personnel and Administrative Reforms, SC representation which should be 15 per cent in all cases is only 6.6 per cent in class I, II. 8 per cent in class II, 14.8 per cent in class III. The quota is filled only in class IV category which includes minial jobs.

Objectives

It is argued that the reservation policy in India seeks to achieve three goals. The first objective is to remove the social and religious disabilities of certain specified groups suffering disabilities because of their social segregation, and spatial and cultural isolation, namely, the Scheduled Castes (SC) and Scheduled Tribes. The second objective, is to facilitate and promote equal participation with others of all socially disadvantaged and disabled groups in organized sectors of the country's economic and political life. This is sought to be achieved through provisions for preferential treatment in education, in government employment reservation of seats in Parliament, State legislatures and local, bodies and through other ameliorative measures and schemes designed to improve their life chances with exception of reservations in legislature, the other preferential measures are not confined only to the SC and ST Communities, they also extend to the category popularly known as the other backward classes (OBC). The third objective is to protect, if necessary, through legislative action and executive orders, all these groups described in the Constitution as weaker sections of society, or simply, the backward classes, from all forms of social injustice and exploitation. Apparently, reservation or the provision of protective discrimination as enshrined in the Constitution, forms part of the policy package which seeks to create a civil society through extension of the effective citizenship rights to the vast mass of population who have been historically deprived and marginalized.

The ruling classes in India had evolved the strategy of making provisions for reservations in the constitution out of political exigency to resolve the challenges that they faced in maintaining their dominance. The Congress recognized as late as 1917 the need 'for removing disabilities imposed on the depressed classes' when they demanded communal representation like that of the Muslims and the Sikhs. The Congress agreed to accommodate the Harijans in the distribution of Assembly and Parliment seats when the British Government offered communal representation to the depressed classes at the Round Table Conference. Initially Gandhiji refused because he feared that the separate electorate would create division among the Hindus.[7] Several tribal groups demanded separate electorate in the 1930's. Some theatened to secede from the Indian Union. Thus the ruling classes accepted reservations not because of the desire to build up an egalitarian social order but because of the pressure exerted by the different minorities.

The reservation policy seeks to benefit three different types of communities : ex-untouchables designated as S.C. (over 104 million), the spatially and culturally isolated communities of tribals designated as S.T. (over 51 million) and the vaguely defined category of the socially and educationally backward classes of citizens called OBC (an estimated 300 million). The OBC is a category consisting of a wide array of groups in need of preferential treatment, but it does not have any centrally identificable systematic features. By and large by OBC is meant those groups of people who are at the lower rungs of the Sudra Castes socially disadvantaged in terms of occupational mobility, and have in the past, suffered from the different degrees of ritual prohibitions.

Benefits

For the SCs and STs reservations are made for seats in the legislatures, government employment and educational institutions, in proportion of their strength in population. For jobs in government services and seats in educational institutions only those who meet certain prescribed minimum standards, qualifo. These standards are determined with reference to the prevailing competitive standards for all except in the case of SC and ST candidates in which cases they are lowered or relaxed to a certain extent.

The constitution is ailent on the question of legislative reservations or reservations in Government jobs and seats in educational institutions in respect of the OBCs. The matter has been left to the discretion of the state Governments. We have, therefore states like West Bengal, Orissa, Assam, and all union territories where there exists no reservation for the OBCs. The States of North India, and Gujarat and Maharashtra have been extending the benefits of reservation to OBC since the mid-seventies. This is however, not the case with the South Indian states where these reservations have been existing in one form or another, for over a century.

The Question of OBC

The question or reservations for the OBC generated a lot heat in the Constituent Assembly. The delegates from the north expressed supprise at the provisions for 'backward classes" in

Article 16(4). The representatives from Madras, Mysore and Bombay argued that the term 'backward. classes' was a distinct term with a technical meaning.[8] K.M. Munshi spoke of the need for a generic term and suggested, "it signifies people—touchable or untouchable, belonging to this community or that—who are so backward that special protection is required in the services."[9] Dr. Ambedkar, defending the draft, explained that a backward community is a community which is backward in opinion of the respective local government. Gallanter observes, "The delegation to local authorities undoubtedly reflected an acceptance (at best temporarily) of the divergence of the existing practices, a desire to preserve flexibility, and an awareness of the difficulties of prescribing universally applicable tests of backwardness in view of the varying local conditions. It may also have been presumed that 'Backward Classes' were sufficiently potent politically to look out for their own interests on a local level, and unlike Scheduled Castes and Scheduled Tribes, Central control over their designation was not required to ensure the inclusion of the deserving.[11] The President is instructed to appoint a Backward Classes Commission to investigate the conditions of socially and educationally backward classes... and the difficulties under which they labour and to make recommendations so as to take steps that should be taken by the Union or any State to remove such difficulties and to improve their conditions". (Article 340).

The Backward Classes Commission was set up in 1950 and directed to "determine the criteria to be adopted in considering whether any sections of the people...(in addition to the Scheduled Castes and Tribes) should be treated as socially and educationally backward classes and in accordance with such criteria, to prepare a list of such classes.[12] The Commission had drawn up a list of

2,399 backward groups and recommended various measures for their economic, social, political, educational and cultural advance ment. The Commission found it difficult to avoid caste in the present prevailing circumstances as a criterion for the determination of backwardness although there were differences of opinion among the members about caste as the criterion. The Chairman himself changed his opinion at the final stage.

The Report of the Commission was criticised on the floor of the Parliament by many including the Minister-in-Charge of Home Affairs because of the emphasis on caste. It was argued that caste criterion was not only administratively unworkable, but was contrary to the first principle of social justice in their unfairness to the other poor. It would be contrary to the Constitution, perpetuate caste and would create in the recipients both vested interests and a sense of helplessness. The Centre endorsed economic criteria, but refrained from enforcing it on the states, preferred the path of persuasion.[13] As the Commission failed to identify positive and workable criteria the matter was left to the state governments.

This resulted in differential policies in different states. For example, while Gujarat provided for 10 per cent reservation of the government jobs to the OBC, it was 14 per cent in Maharashtra, 15 per cent in Uttar Pradesh, and 14 per cent in Himachal Pradesh. The upper and the middle castes began to feel insecure in the mid seventies when many states in North India, and the States of Gujarat and Maharashtra started providing reservations for the OBC. The upper and middle castes launched agitation against the reservations for SC, ST and OBC in Gujarat, Madhya Pradesh and Andhra. The dominant castes oppose reservation on various grounds. And wherever possible they try to sabotage the implementation of reservation orders. One can refer to a number of delaying tactics on the part of the upper caste officers in implementing reservation orders. The Commissioner for SC and ST observed in its 24th Report (1976-77) that out of the total number of 151 ST vacancies proposed for reservation in 1974, S.T. candidates available for as many as 254 vacancies for class III posts, possessing the minimum qualifications laid down for the posts were declared unsuitable for appointment. Ghanashyam Shah observes that the caste bias is reflected in the attitude of the trade unions also.

The conflict between the dominant and the deprived castes has been taken to the High Courts and Supreme Court also. There were 113 litigation cases about compensatory discrimination from 1950 to 1977. And significantly, as Gallanter observes, "no judge has emerged as the champion of compensatory discrimination, Justice (later Chief Justice) Ganjendra Gadkar probably comes closest by virtue of his opinion in *Dora* and *Rangachari*, two of the small number of the Supreme Courts' cases in which the scope of preferential treatment was given a broadening, expensive interpretation. A few other judges sat often enough to display a consistent tendency to curtail its operation"[14].

In 1978 the Central Government had appointed the Second Backward classes Commission which, in its report submitted in 1980, recommended central action in regard to reservations for the OBCs assigining the centre the role it plays vis-a-vis the SCs and STs. The Commission used caste as a criterion for the determination of social and educational backwardness of the groups of potential beneficiaries and submitted a long list of 3,743 backward castes. The population of the other backward classes thus included was around 52 per cent of the total population. But to keep the total reservations for all categories within the limit of 50% prescribed by the Supreme Court, the Commission recommended only 27% reservations for the OBCs. The South Indian states which had already made reservations above 27%, however, remained unaffected.

The Commission also considered the arguments against caste-based reservations. Some of the frequently advanced arguments are :

(a) Only small portion of the total number of classes for which the policy was envisaged would benefit on account of the limited scope for employment in government ;

(b) an elite will develop among the backward classes who will monopolise the jobs so reserved ;

(c) meritorious students from other classes will suffer on account of policy ; and

(d) the efficiency of the administrative services will suffer once they are packed with personnel who get in on a basis other than merit.

Refuting these arguments the Report observes that the essential battle against backwardness has to be fought in the minds of the members of the backward classes. It is argued that the government service commands considerable power and prestige. What is, therefore, necessary is to develop an awareness among the members of the backward communities that they can aspire for it. Secondly, the entry on merit does not ensure against upper caste officers being inefficient or corrupt. The report alludes to the prospect of officers from the backward classes being more attuned to the needs of development. Thirdly, against the argument that the reservation policy harms the interests of the meritorious students the Commission suggests, "what we call merit in an elitist society is an amalgam of native endowments and environmental privileges".

There are some other liberal scholars who oppose reservation in government employment because the reservation beneficiaries will not be efficient because they are less meritorious. It is argued that economic growth is also hampered as a result of reservation policy which does not take merit into account. It is also observed that the present administrative inefficiency in government organisation is the result of the reservation policy which facilitates entry of the less qualified persons in government services.

It has to be borne in mind that efficiency and merit do not always go together. It is the professional commitment and professionalism which largely determine the efficiency of the government servants. Padma Velaskor's study of Bombay medical students shows that SC/OBC students have more commitment towards the profession and the poor people than those who belong to the dominant castes.[15]

The dominant propaganda that the system of reservations has created an elite among the SC and ST is unfounded. For example, in the Supreme Court there has been only one SC judge even after four decades of reservation. In all the High Courts taken together there were only five judges as on 19 April 1979. In the state higher judicial services the all India representation of SC is 2.1 per cent and ST 0.24 per cent. In the state judicial services the corresponding figures are 7 and

0.84 per cent. These figures are actually overestimates because they exclude major High Courts such as Bombay, Karnataka, Madhya Pradesh and Patna which have either refused to implement any reservation at all even for menial posts, or agreed to implement it only partially.[16]

The general feature of reservations is that they have been considerably implemented in the lower sections of the working class, class IV employees and the like. In the working class the lower castes are largely confined to the hard jobs and menial jobs. In the class III employees, clerical staff reservations have been partially implemented, as is also the case with skilled workers. Coming to the officer level of class I and II the surface of the upper caste domination has barely been scratched. The situation is even worse in the professions.

In the public sector for which reservation was made in mid 60s, there were only 1.4 per cent SC and 0.6 per cent ST officers in Class I position in 1975. The figures rose to 2, 4 and 16 per cent for SC and 0.47, 0.97 and 7.41 per cent for S.T. in class I, II and III respectively in 1978. A 1971 survey of Indian managers showed that only one per cent among them came from all three categories of the backward classes taken together. In the North Indian states and in Gujarat and Maharashtra the utilization of reservation in government services and educational institutions by the OBC is much less than the allocation made for. For example, in Gujarat against 10 per cent reservation the utilisation of seats in the Engineering and Medical Colleges is 4 per cent and 5 per cent respectively.[17]

The SC-ST leaders have secured position in the legislature. But the legislators have failed to participate actively in the debate in the state assemblies or the Parliament concerning the issues affecting the deprived communities.[18] The SC members of Parliament could not effectively pressurize the Parliament to pass without delay the Untouchability (Offences) Act. The Parliament took five years to pass such an Act. Ghanashyam Shah observes "The SC-ST MLAs and MPs do use their numerical strength as a block power in faction ridden party politics and they work as a balancing forces between the two rival actions. In return for their support to one or another faction, they bargain for political positions in the Cabinet or various committees or statutory bodies. But they cannot act effectively when the atrocities are committed against members of their communities ; nor do they pressurize the administration for the implementation of minimum wages or distribution of land."[19]

The reservation policy has been criticised by a number of scholars, namely, Marc Gallanter, Barbara Joshi, Karuna Ahmed and others. It is argued that the reservation on caste basis provides fuel to the rise of casteism in Indian politics and dampens the process of secularisation of Indian society. To Barnabas and Mehta reservation on the basis of caste...has affected the morals, the administration and society adversely. The attempt to atone for the injustice perpetuated on the lower castes in times past has in effect become a tool of aggrandisement in the hands of the numerically large and hence politically dominant caste groups in majority of states.[20] B.A.V. Sharma has suggested that the very foundations of secularism have been undermined by the prepetuation and accentuation of caste consciousness as a result of caste being considered as a criterion for the governmental definition of backwardness.[21] It invokes caste feeling and strengthens caste consciousness. It is assumed that casticism was not strong before the introduction of reservation. It is also assumed that the members of the upper castes are benevolent, tolerant and secular.

Ghanshyam Shah refuses to accept this approach. He says that there was no reservation for the OBCs in many states including Gujarat till the mid-seventies.[22] But even a cursory analysis of Gujarat politics would show that before 1976 caste consciousness was as strong as it was before the introduction of reservation for the OBCs in 1978. Secondly, the upper castes are secular as long as their monopoly is maintained, and they are allowed to share the benefit among themselves.

Some scholars like Gallanter, Chetkar Jha oppose the reservation policy on the ground that it endangers the processes of national integration by creating disharmony among the 'different section of the Indian society.'

This view does not appear to be sound. The fact appears to be otherwise. The reservation policy can play an effective role in national integration by helping the SC and ST and OBC to join the national mainstream.

The reservation policy has come in for sharp criticism in the hands of the communal organizations like the Rastriya Swayam Sevak Sangha, the Maratha Mahasangha (Maharashtra), Palit Pawan Sangha (Gujarat). The basic contention of the communal organizatons is that the reservation policy has resulted in growing unemplopment among the high caste young people.

The Marxists generally support reservation policy in India under the existing socio-economic conditions. But they strongly argue that caste system which constitutes the basis of reservation, has to be eradicated at all costs. Caste-based reservation policy as it leads to inner conflict among the toiling masses, needs to be replaced by economic backwardness. Secondly, caste in India is utilised by the ruling classes as vote bank. This aspects has also been emphasised by the liberal pluralist scholars like Myron Weiner, Rajni Kothari and others.

Gopal Guru has identified some functions which the reservation policy performs. First, most of the reservation beneficiaries are being bourgeoisified as they are imbibing the bourgeois moral principle. The bourgeoisified middle class from the reservation beneficiaries starts disassociating itself from its sombre masses and associates with the bourgeois framework. Secondly, the role of bourgeoisified middle class in democracy and legislature has been disappointing in so far as the upliftment of the respective communities is concerned. They become part of the ruling class and provide and protect their interests either through being almost quiet in the legislature or taking up issues which hardly relate to the common interests. Reservations in jobs and education have made some headway, but not very much of a difference to the agrarian position of the *dalits*. A considerable section of the upper castes has become rich peasants. This will be evident from the growing importance of a section of the upper caste like Jadavs and Kurmis in Bihar and Uttar Pradesh—in the electrol politics. But this is not "the same thing as saying that they have become integrated into the ruling classes. They seem to have been able to pose a challenge to the upper castes which is determind to maintain its domination. The recent spate of anti-reservation campaigns in Bihar, U.P. etc. can be understood in the light of this situation."[25] Thirdly, the reservation policy diffuses the problem of unemployment by creating a conflicting situation horizontaly and vertically. At horizontal level it fans hostilities between SC and non SC. At vertical level it creates an air of tension among the SC people. Unemployment is the product of the path of development India has chosen.

Reservation policy has a great merit in our class divided caste ridden society, as it seeks to offer discriminininatory treatment to those who are placed at the lower rungs in the social ladder. Reservation policy has a progressive feature in the sense that it seeks to homogenize the class structure of the various castes. But the problem is that the rate at which homogenization of class structure takes place, depends very much upon the overall rate of social transformation which is not something affected by reservation alone.

It has to be kept in mind that we have a very large private sector where there is no reservation. The public sector in our country is very small. If the state in India is really serious of improving the lot of the down-and-out, it should compel the private sector to adopt the policy of reservation in employment. Given the class character of the Indian state it is but a day dream.

The principal objective of reservation policy is to emancipate the poor people from the trap of exploitation and to integrate them into the national mainstream. But the question is that the state in India has been caputred by the bourgeoisie which is sharing power with the feudallords. Caste which is considered the basis of reservation, is perpetuated by the state. It is rooted in the feudal mode of production which has been co-existing with the capitalist mode in India. The ruling classes in India cannot launch a battle for emancipating the poor from exploitation because they themselves constitute the exploiter class. How then can the reservations policy achieve the objective it stands for ? Reservation policy to be effective, has therefore, to be combined with an attack against the existing power structure.

REFERENCES

1. Eleanor Zealot, "Learning the use of Political Means, the Mahars of Maharashtra" in R. Kothari, (ed.) *Caste in Indian Politics*, Orient Longman, New Delhi, 1970, p. 33.

2. N. Pandit, Caste and Class in Maharashtra *Economic and Political Weekly*, (EPW) Annual Number, February, 1979, p. 427.

3. T.V. Satyamurthy, The Dravida Munnetra Kazhagham in the Politics of Tamil Nadu, 1949-1971 in B.N. Pandey, (ed.) *Leadership in South Asia*, Vikas Publishing House, New Delhi, 1977, p. 430.

4. Louis Dumont, *Religion, Politics and History in India*, Mouton, Paris, 1977, p. 99.

5. Gail Omvedt, *Cultural Revolt in Colonial Society—The Non-Brahmin Movement in Western India*, Scientific Socialist Education Trust, Bombay, 1976, p. 23.

6. See Ghanashyam Shah, The Congress and the Deprived Committees' in Ram Joshi and R K. Hebsur (eds.), *Social Intervention for Justice*, Popular Prakashan, 1980.

7. See 'Eleanor Zellot, 'Gandhi and Ambedkar A Study in Leadership in Michael Mahar (ed.), *The Untouchables in Contemporary India*, Tuscon the University of Arizona Press, 1972.

8. *Constituent Assembly Debates*, Vol. II, pp. 689-92.

9. *Ibid.*, p. 697.

10. Ibid., Vol. III, p. 702.

11. Marc Gallenter, 'Who are the other Backward Classes ? : An Introduction to a Conrtitutional Puzzle' *EPW*, October 28, 1978, p. 1814.

12. *Ibid*, p. 1817.

13. *Lok Sabha Debates*, series 3, Vol. 48, pp 3973-75, November 25, 1965.

14. Marc Gallanter, *Competing Inequalities*, OUP, Delhi, 1984.

15. P.R. Velaskar, *Inequality in Higher Education : A Study of Scheduled Caste Students in Medical Colleges of Bombay*, TISC, 1986.

16. *Report of the Commissioner for Scheduled Castes and Tribes*, Manager, Government of India Press, New Delhi, 1979-81, Part I.

17. See D.L. Seth 'Reservation Policy Revisited, paper presented at the Seminar on *Reservations, Objectives and Politics*, under the auspices of Centre for Policy Research, New Delhi during March 18-20, 1987.

18. See G. Shah, 'Protective Discrimination : Equality and Political Will in *Reservation : Policy, Programmes and Issues* (ed.) V. Shah, & B.C. Agarwal, Rawat Publications, Jaipur, 1980.

19. See G. Shah, 'Consequences of Reservation' Paper presented at the Seminar, *op. cit.*

20. A.P. Barnabas and S.C. Mehta, *Caste in Changing India*, Indian Institute of Public Administration, New Delhi, 1965, pp. 76-77.

21. B.A.V. Sharma, 'Secular State and Civil Servi.e' in *Secularism in India*, (ed), V.K. Sinha, Lalvani, Bombay, 1968, p. 70.

22. G. Shah, 'Consequences of Reservation', *op. cit.*

23. Gopal Guru, 'Politics of Reservation : A Class Approach', *Society and Change*, Vol. IV, No. 3, April-June, 1985.

24. N. Pandit, *op. cit.*, p. 47.

25. D.N., 'Reservations and Class Structure of Castes', *EPW*, January 13, 1990.

CHAPTER 6

From Ethnicity to Regionalism : The Jharkhand Agitation

Jharkhand literally means an 'area of the jungles' and forms part of what is known as the central-cum-eastern Indian tribal belt. This belt comprises, mainly, some portions of Orissa (the districts of Koraput, Mayurbhang and Sundergarh), Madhya Pradesh (Bastar, Surguga and Raigarh), some portions of West Bengal (Jalpaiguri, Darjeeling, 24-Parganas, Nadia, Midnapore, Purulia, Burdwan and Coach-behar) and some portions of Bihar (Ranchi, Hazaribagh, Singhbhum, Santhal Parganas, Palamau, Dhanbad and Giridih). Out of this central-cum-eastern Indian tribal belt the area known as Jharkhand consists of the tribal areas of Madhya Pradesh, Orissa, Bihar and the Western areas of West Bengal.

Out of about 3 crore population of the Jharkhand region one crore belong to tribals and sixty lakhs, Harijans. The total percentage of Scheduled Castes and Scheduled Tribes constitute about 47% which is bigger than the national average of 22%. The Oraons, Mundas, Hos and the Santhals are the major tribal communities inhabiting the region. Among the Scheduled Castes Bowri, Mochi, Rajwar, Dhobi, Bhiya are the main categories. In addition, major inhabitants of the region included Nag, Shadhan, Kurmi, Momins etc. who constitute the lower strata of the backward caste mainly placed with the Harijans.

The heart of Jharkhand is the Chhotanagpur region which was made habitable mainly by the Mundas and Oraons. They were reported to have a homogeneous social order in which land was held in common, and each and every capable person took part in the processes of production. The villages known as Khuntkali (land of the original settlers) were characterised by a very high degree of simplicity and economic self-sufficiency.

The Chhotanagpur – Santhal Parganas region is said to have been known as Jharkhand in ancient times. Around the middle age the Nag tribe came from the north, and settled in this region establishing a small kingdom. The attention of the Mughals was drawn to this region in the 16th century when diamonds were unearthed from Chhotanagpur. In the battle of 1657 Jhangir defeated the tribal army, and seized all stocks of diamonds, and demanded an annual tribute from the ruler. But the ruler failed to pay the tribute as a result of which a war took place in 1670 culminating in the capture and detention of the tribal king.

Following this triumph, the way of life of the tribals underwent a major change. With the inroduction of the Mughal land revenue system the ruling Nag tribe invited Muslims and upper caste Hindus from North Bihar. The Brahmins came as priests, the Kayastha as officials and Rajputes and Muslims as military personnel. The Nag rulers conferred lands on the Hindu migrants with a view to strengthening their feudal base.

The advent of the East India Company added a new dimension to the social composition and economic exploitation of the Adivasis. The Chhotanagpur region along with the adjoining areas was known as Khukhra before the British took over the administration of the area in 1765. The British renamed it as the Ramgarh Hill Tract. A century later it was re-designated as South West Frontier Agency, although it continued to be administered as part of Bengal. In 1854 the Chhotanagpur Division was set up within the province of Bengal. The Biharis demanded a separate province, and the Province of Bihar was separated from Bengal, and at that time Bihar, Chhotanagpur and Orissa were yoked together to constitute a separate State—Bihar.

While most of the Chhotanagpur Division became part of the combined province of Bihar and Orissa three districts-Midnapore, Purulia and Santhal Parganas—remained with Bengal. In 1930 Orissa was again separated and Chhotanagpur alone remained with Bihar. The Chhotanagpur region further shrank in size when four districts—Mayurbhang, Koraput, Sundergarh and Sambalpur were joined with Central Provinces. In this way the homogeneous Central and Eastern Indian tribal belt broke into four parts.

The Chhotanagpur Unnati Samaj was the first formal organisation established with the support of all tribal groups. When the era of constitutional reforms began, and the demands for the promotion and protection of regional interests grew, the educated Christian tribals organised this Samaj at the instance of the

Anglican Bishop of Ranchi. The Samaj had two objectives, namely : (a) upliftment of Chhotanagpur from its backward status, (b) improvement of the social, economic and political conditions of the adivasis. These objectives received wide publicity through the Magazine known as *Adivasi.* The Samaj tried to strengthen the bond of tribal solidarity in the region, though it was essentially a welfare organisation. There was not yet any idea for a separate tribal state. The Samaj was able to focus the attention of the authorities on the problems of the tribes. The Simon Commission and the Government paid some attention to the tribal problems, and sought their solutions within the framework of the existing political structure.

However, the Samaj was a short lived organisation. Torn by internal disunity and discord it suffered a tremendous erosion of strength, and became organisationally weak with the formation of the Kishan Sabha and Catholic Sabha. The former was dominated by the tribal converts to Christianity and latter by the non-convert adivasis. In 1937 elections the Kishan Sabha fared badly, and nothing has been heard of it since then.

In 1930, particularly after the Home Rule was introduced, there came up new political opportunities for the Indian masses including tribals. The elites in the backward communities realised that they could utilize the situation in their favour by working as parties or pressure groups. In 1935 the Chhotanagpur and Santhal Pargana region was declared 'partially excluded areas.' This provided the tribal elites an opportunity to organise themselves.

In 1938 an organisation known as the Adivasi Mahasabha was set up under the leadership of Theodore Surin, an advocate. It succeeded Unnati Samaj. The immediate cause of the formation of this Mahasabha was the experience of the first elections held in 1937 under the Government of India Act, 1935. The Congress swept the polls. This pursuaded Christian as also non-Christian tribals to get together. The Chhotanagpur Unnati Samaj and other organisations thus merged to form the Adivasi Mahasabha.

One year after its formation Jaipal Singh became the President of the Mahasabha. It was led by professional political workers. K.S. Singh says, "It became Chhotanagpur movement extending over both urban and rural areas."[1] Jaipal Singh made efforts to evoke what may be called primordial sentiments of the tribals to unite them. He tried to universalise the cause of the Jharkhand statehood by including non-adivasis of the region as members of the Mahasabha.

The Adivasi Mahasabha in its Jamshedpur session held on 20-21 January, 1939 resolved that in order to broaden the base of the movement a political party of tribals and non-tribals was to be formed. This decision may be said to have led to the birth of the Jharkhand Party in 1945. Two other important factors which contributed to the formation of this Party were the experiences of the militant movements, and the framing of the Indian Constitution. The Fifth and the Sixth Schedule of the Indian Constitution recognised the tribals as a minority. The Mahasabha organised a series of violent incidents for realising the demand for a sub state to be separated from Bihar.

Following K.S. Singh it can be said that during the pre-Independence days the movement passed through three phases. The first phase which lasted up to 1920, "saw the rise of the institutions designed to introduce reforms and stimulate the development among the tribals mainly along denominational and partly along inter-denominational lines." The leadership was provided by the Christian students and missionaries. In 1906 there came the Catholic Co-operative Society. The objective of this Society was to 'civilise' the aboriginals, and raise their standards of life generally. In 1912 the Chhotanagpur Charitable Association was organised by all aboriginals, Christians and non-Christians to raise funds for the students. At that time a new sentiment-a pan-tribal sentiment was gaining ground.

Another significant landmark of this phase was the organisation of the Chhotanagpur Improvement Society at the instance of the Anglican Bishop of Ranchi. The Society was concerned with the economic advancement of tribal community. But by 1920 the Society became more or less moribund.

The second phase began in 1920 and lasted upto 1938. The most important development of this phase was the revival of the Improvement Society. At that time tribal middle class was being born, and this class was trying to provide leadership for organising movement in order to secure employment for educated tribals and ensure formation of a substate joined to Bengal or Orissa. The Improvement Society did make some progress by drawing attention of the authorities to tribal problems.

The third phase of the movement began in 1938 and lasted upto 1947. This phase was dominated by the militant activities of the Adivasi Mahasabha. The Mahasabha extended its hands of co-operation beyond the domain of the Ranchi tribals, and tried to spread its tentacles in the rural areas. But in the elections held in 1946 the Mahasabha was routed by Congress.

In the elections held in 1952 the Jharkhand Party emerged as the major party in the Chhotanagpur Parganas region. However, the Party pleaded before the States Re-organisation Commission (SRC) for a separate state comprising 16 districts—7 from Bihar, 3 from West Bengal, 4 from Orissa and 2 from Madhya Pradesh. The memorandum runs thus : "Jharkhand is not a natural part of Bihar. It has an administrative status of its own. It is a unity by itself...." The Party organised a massive demonstration of over 40,000 people in support of its demand when the Commission was visiting Ranchi in 1955. But the SRC turned down the plea for a separate Jharkhand state by giving three arguments. The tribals are in a minority in the region. There is no specific link language in the regions and the economic balance of the region would be disturbed if a separate Jharkhand state was set up.

Since the late 50s the party started getting disorganised. Internal dissidence within the party was surfacing. The agrarian situation was deteriorating. But the party could not stand up to the expectations. The non-Christian tribals started looking mainly to the Congress or the Jan Sangha for support among the many all-India parties that appeared on the scene.

In 1962 elections the party suffered a great debacle. In 1963 the Jharkhand Party was merged with the Congress. This merger shocked the hard core of the Jharkhandis and sections of the dominant Christian elite and elite and missionaries who feared loss of leverage they exercised. The merger was not ratified by the general body. As many as nine groups appeared to fill the vaccum created by the merger. During the years 1963-1968 three factions claimed to represent the party.

Since 70s the Party began steadily losing its grip over the masses. It did not contest the Lok-Sabha poll in 1977. In the election to the Bihar Assembly in May 1977 all four splinter groups of the Party polled only 81,227 votes. The Janta wave swept the tribal regions.

The Jharkhand movement gathered some momentum in October 1977. It reached its culmination in the Ranchi Bandh on 12 May, 1978. In its conference held on 21 May, 1978 the All India Jharkhand Party declared that if the demand for a separate state was not conceded by 15 August, 1978 it would begin a non-co-operation movement.

The demand was not realised. This led the Jharkhand Party to launch direct action programmes like organising bandhs, dharnas etc. But the direct action programmes failed as a result of which the Jharkhand Party switched over to the political action, and called a Conference of the regional parties at Jamshedpur on 20th to evolve a strategy. Many groups came together to demand a separate Jharkhand state, and formed a common platform with its own flag in September 1978.

In 1979 the Jharkhand Party released a document[2] showing the geographic and demographic features of the proposed Jharkhand state. The proposed state will have an area of 1,07,646 Sq. Kilometres. Its population according to 1971 census was estimated to be 25,984,748. The community-wise break-up is as follows :

Tribals	9,239,769
Scheduled Castes	3,752,605
Non-Tribals (non-scheduled and non-exploitative communities living in Jharkhand for fairly long time)	12, 9 ,374
Total	25,984,748

(The non-tribal population consists of those who have been living in Jharkhand since ancient times plus those Marwari, Bengali, Oriya, Punjabi and Gujrati traders who came to Jharkhand several decades ago and today consider themselves Jharkhandis. These figures do not include migrant industrial workers from North Bihar).

In the early seventies rose the Jharkhand Mukti Morcha (JMM) with the objective of forming a separate tribal state, ending exploitation of tribals by non-tribals and securing preferential treatment for the sons of the soil in the matter of employment. This was the second phase of the movement. The leader of this party is Sibu Soren whose father was killed by village Mahajan in 1957. This event shaped Sibu's future. As a youth he joined the Jharkhand movement led by Jaipal Singh. Singh's defection to the Congress disappointed him. The J.M.M. has its support base among the Santhals and Hos. It has also the support of the Mahato-Kurmis. The separate tribal state to which the J.M.M. is committed, comprises 15 districts—6 from Bihar, 3 from West Bengal, 4 from Orrissa and 2 from Madhya Pradesh. The Morcha gained ground in the industrial belt of Dhanbad, and has been trying to spread its network in the adjoining districts of West Bengal and Orrissa. According to it the Jharkhand is an 'internal colony' which is being exploited by outsiders. The development process itself is exploitative of the local inhabitants. There is a Jharkhand nationality, and as in all nationality questions self-determination is the key element in the social formation. For the satisfactory solution of the nationality question a separate state is a *sine-qua non.* The Jharkhand should, therefore, turn into *Lalkhand.* The movement of political separatism and struggle of the working classes should go together. Ever since its founding the Morcha had been celebrating 4 February as the Jharkhand Day.

The J.M.M. emerged as a major political force in industrial mining belt in Chhotanagpur particularly since 1980s general election. It captured 13 seats while the Jharkhand Party could beg only one seat. The Morcha set about mobilising the peasants against the money lenders. Village Tribal Committees were formed at the initiative of the Morcha. These Committees declared a moratorium on all debts, freed the villagers from the clutches of the ususers, and harvested the crops raised by them on the mortgaged land. The Morcha cadres made a serious attempt at conscientizing the villagers by running night schools. They were taght how they could fight against their continued miseries. The Morcha gathered strength when the Marxist—Co-ordination Committee (MCC) joined the Morcha. During the Emergency many Morcha leaders were put behind the bars. The Morcha Committee, however, survived.

But after the Emergency the vested interests could manage to join the Morcha. The famous zamindars like Basant Narain Singh who earlier opposed the movement became members of the Morcha. It was followed by alienation of a section of the peasantry from the working class. The old slogan against all outsiders was heard again. N. Sengupta is of the opinion that the cause of this re-emergence of this slogan is to be sought in the propaganda tirade of the Patna Press (owned by the upper class landlord) and the infitration of alien class interests into the movement.

The matter came to a head before the 1980 elections. One faction led by Sibu Soren joined the Congress (I) camp while the other led by Roy maintains its left identity. Sibu Soren made a tactical withdrawal from the movement in the interests of his new ally. In fact he became close to the industrialists, contractors, businessmen and the bureaucrats.

The movement reached the third phase in 1987 when the JCC was formed. The JCC is made of diverse groups representing about 62 organisations. The J.C.C. which is the apex body coodinating the activities of the various Jharkhand factions says that the demand for a separate state is not a demand of the santhals and adivasis alone. Nor is the agitation only aimed at securing redressal for the fruits of development. The JCC claims that for the people it is a 'nationality question.' It is a demand of all the people residing in the Jharkhand area. And this demand can only be met by achieving autonomy in the form of a state. The tribal homeland as envisioned by the JCC comprises 21 districts of four states. Twelve of the districts are in Bihar : Singbhum, Ranchi, Giridih, Lohardaga, Gumla, Palamau, Hazaribagh, Dhanbad, Dhumka, Godda, Deoghar, and Sahabganj ; four in Orrissa : Mayurbhang, Keonghar, Sambalpur, Sundargarh and three in West Bengal : Purulia, Midnapore and Bankura and two in Madhya Pradesh : Surjuga and Rajgarh. The total area is 187,646 square kilometres and the total population of the Jharkhand area is 35,098,991.

The most important characteristic feature of this phase is the participation of the tribal intellectuals and students in the movements. The students organised themselves under the All Jharkhand Students Union (AJSU) in October 1986. They may have been encouraged to organize themselves following the success of the All Assam Students Union in wrestling political power after a long drawn struggle in Assam. The students seized the leadership. The phase of the movement is also marked by a conspicuous lack of tribal chauvinism. Surprisingly enough this phase witnessed the phenomenon of the Christian-non-christian divide. The Viswa Hindu Parishad and Rastriya Savamsevak

Sangha are now active to bring the tribals into the Hindu fold and thus expand their base in the area.

Policy Responses

The attention of the Government of India to the problems in the Jharkhand region was drawn in the early 70s. The Government set up two autonomous development authorities in Chhotanagpur and Santhal Parganas regions. But nothing worth mentioning has come up. The Government appointed the Haimed Committee to suggest measures for the improvement of the functioning of these authorities. But the Committee report has not been implemented. In 1975 the Mrs. Gandhi Government appointed a Cabinet Sub-Committe to look into the matter. The Tribal Advisory Committee was reconstituted in 1984. But it has done absolutely nothing to benefit the tribals. When the movements gathered considerable momentum during the regime of Rajive Gandhi, his Government constituted a committee consisting of the representatives of the Centre, Bihar Government and the Jharkhand Movement. The Committee, as reported in the newspaper, submitted a report which has not yet been made public.

The Chhotanagpur plateau is Jharkhand's dominating geographical feature and a heaven of Adivasis for centuries. It covers a meagre 2.5 per cent of India's area but holds 25 per cent of its mineral wealth. 72 per cent of copper deposits, 52 per cent of mica, 48.6 per cent of coal and 38.4 per cent of bauxite, huge deposits of iron ore, uranium, asbestos, fire clay, manganese ore, nickel, kyanite, lead and zinc.[3] Such a prosperous region continued to remain among the least developed in India until the middle of the 19th century. In 1956 coal mining was developed in Dhanbad district with coal-fields at Jharia, Bokaro, and

Karanpura. The British discovered that the region was rich with minerals and soon thereafter Chhotanagpur became a major producer of minerals.

The easy availability of coal, iron and other metals has led to rapid industrialisation. At Sindri there came up a huge fertiliser factory. In 1906 Tata created the Tata Iron and Steel Company at Jamshedpur which produces a substantial quantum of iron and steel in the continent.

Huge manufacturing complexes have also grown up alongside the extractive industries. After Independence there developed an industrial complex at Hatia. Nearly one fifth of India's total public sector investments in industrial activities are located in the region.

Industrialisation has, however, forced the local tribal people to leave their homes. With the establishment of the industrial complex at Hatia vast tracts of tribal lands were acquired by the Heavy Engineering Corporation. During the First Five Year Plans more than 50,000 Scheduled Tribe families and 10,000 Scheduled Castes families in Jharkhand had to leave their homes for making lands available for the construction of public sector industrial projects alone. The efforts of the Government received a greater momentum after the first three plans were over because such gigantic projects as Bokaro Steel or Patrau or Tenughat Super Thermal Power Plants came up thereafter.

Thus industrialisation has led to a massive up-rooting of tribals from the soil to pave the way for development. In front of the eyes of 5 lakh tribals of Orissa, for example, 18 lakh houses came up for the workers of the Rourkela Steel Plant and Hirakud

Multipurpose Project, while they were rendered homeless.[4] We find from the Annual Report of Industrial and Commercial Undertakings of the Central Government 1973-74 that out of a total of 2,80,000 quarters constructed throughout the country for workers in the public sector projects no less than 60,000 are located in this small region. The uprooting of tribals has also taken place as a result of construction of dams for irrigation and hydro-electric projects. For example, the Koel-Karo Hydro Electric Project, the construction of which has been stalled by the tribal resistance since 1981 will mean the eviction and near submergence of about 50 villages, the loss of 26,000 acres of cultivable land, and 14,000 acres of uncultivated land.

Besides, only a small number of local tribal people found employment in the industries. In a Study of the Heavy Engineering Corporation it was found that in one plant only 335 workers out of 4,284 were tribals.[5] The workers even for unskilled jobs, were recruited from outside. Nirmal Sengupta says that approximately 10 per cent immigrants in Jharkhand appropriate more than 50 per cent of the industrial jobs.[6] There are provisions of 80% reservations for tribal and local people in training and jobs, but the fact is that nearly 80% of the training facilities and jobs are enjoyed by outsiders. The basic objective of the reservation policy of the Government is to encourage the weaker sections to catch up with the rest of the people in Indian society. The vested interest groups are active to frustrate the effort of the Government. The most frequently used play to discourage implementation of the reservation policy is to declare the said category of candidates not available. This is followed by deservation which facilitates the appointment of a favoured candidate. Sengupta says, "The Jharkhand benefits from the development of the region in the same manner as the growth of slums is also included in urban development. Among the urban population the Jharkhandis are predominantly slum dwellers ; the immigrants prosperous urban folk. In industrial employment the unskilled workers are Jharkhandis, the well-paid workers one outsiders. The officers came from North Bihar, their orderlies may be Jharkhandis. The contractors are outsiders, the labourers are recriuted locally, the traders, and merchants are Punjabi, Gujrati or Marwari. The professionals are outsiders, the maid-servant's job is a monopoly of the Jharkhandis."[7]

The table below provides a picture of the employment position of the Scheduled Caste and Scheduled Tribes Communities in the different spheres of employment :

	No. of Worker		*Percentage of SC & ST to Total Workers*
	Total	*SC/ST*	
Mining & Quarrying	2,50,104	79,912	32
Household Industry	1,12,295	40,151	36
Other than household industry	2,13,748	43,241	20
Construction	42,275	10,500	25
Trade and Commerce	145,100	6,781	5
Transport etc	1,02,620	23,815	23
Other Services	2,45,026	65,131	27

Source : N. Sengupta 'Class and Tribe in Jharkhand' in *Economic and Political Weekly*, 5 April, 1980.

It should be mentioned that nationalisation has played havoc with the employment of the indigenous tribal population. For example, in a single week following nationalisation of coal mines in 1971 nearly 50,000 Jharkhandi miners lost their jobs, and were replaced by people mainly from Bhojpur region.[9] Significantly, mining was a low-paid job before nationalisation and the Jharkhandis shared these jobs. After nationalisation wages registered an impressive increase, but the Jharkhandis were thrown out of jobs.

Nationalisation of coal brought further miseries to the Jharkhandis. The retrenched employees had to dispose of their lands in order to survive during the period of unemployment. As the labour supply became abundant the landlords further exploited them by reducing wage-rates. Nationalisation also closed the avenues of seasonal migration to coal mines which was an important subsidiary occupation.

It is necessary to note here that the 'development' of the region has brought in outsiders from the different corners of the country. The influx of an outside population has led to the 60 : 40 tribal non-tribal population ratio to become 40 : 60 in 1981. There has been a growing increase in the number of outsiders as is evident from the table below :

Group	*1951*	*1961*
Punjabis	30,000	57,000
Marwaris	8,000	22,000
Gujratis	8,000	36,000
Andhrites	18,000	36,000
Tamils	6,000	15,000
Bengali-Speaking people	702,000	907,000

Source : The Census Report, 1961.

This large number of outsiders (called 'dikus' by the local people) who has settled in the region, control the economy. Taking advantage of the material backwardness of the tribal people migrants have gradually captured the positions of power, and gained control over the business activities. Punjabis have grabbed the transport system, and the Marwaris and Gujratis have gained control over the wholesale and retail trade.

Speaking of the nature of development A. Roy says, "the development of the area does not mean the development of the people from there and replacement by descending the colonies of developed people, the clever people. the politically connected people decending from the developed areas. As the industrialisation of British India was done to drain the resources of the country...so was the industrialisation of Chhotanagpur Jharkhand area where Railways came as early as 1894 to draw out its coal and iron.[10]

Industrialisation has brought with it rapid urbanisation. The towns of Ranchi, Jamshedpur, Singbhum and Dhanbad have all physically expanded into the surrounding countryside. In the past decade Jamesedpur has grown by 42 per cent, Ranchi by 116 percent, and each has physically encroached countryside.

The number of towns in Chhotanagpur—Santhal Parganas has increased from 13 in 1901 to 34 in 1951 and 96 in 1971. The total urban population in the Jharkhand region has increased from 13 lakhs in 1961 to 23 lakhs in 1971.

But the residents of the urban areas are not the 'Jharkhandis' but 'dikus'. In 1971 out of the total urban population in Jharkhand area only 17 percent were Scheduled Castes and

Scheduled Tribes. About 99 percent of the Santhals still live in villages. The Oraons with 5 percent of their total population as urban, rank the highest among the Scheduled Tribes in the degree of urbanisation. Some of the Scheduled Castes, namely, Dasadh, Bauri, Dhobi, Dom, and Ghasi are, however, more urbanised—between 10 to 17 per cent of their population live in urban areas.

The economy of Chhotanagpur is characterised by what may be called 'dualism'. The modern sector is in the hands of the outsiders, while the traditional, marginal agrarian sector remains predominantly local. Large parts of the land area in Jharkhand are covered by forests. The table below shows the land-use pattern.'

Type of land	*Jharkhand*	*Rest of Bihar*	*All India*
Uncultivable	10.7	5.2	13.1
Cultivable follow	7.1	1.2	6.6
Current follow	15.3	8.2	4.9
Other follow	12.0	2.3	3.9
Land put to agricultural use	42.8	68.8	57.8
Land put to non-agricultural use	12.1	14.2	13.6

Source : N. Sengupta 'Caste and Tribe in Jharkhand', EPW, April 5, 1980.

Agriculture is still the mainstay of the tribals. Of the 15,84,907 tribal population of Ranchi district, according to 1981

Census 4,60,234 are cultivators. In the entire State of Bihar 63.06% of the tribals are cultivators. Another 23.20% are agricultural labourers. With 9.2% literacy rate, half the average of Bihar, the tribals are not equipped for any other livelihood but agriculture. But the infrastructure for agricultural development is pitiably inadequate. Because of the lack of adequate irrigation facilities multiple-cropping is yet to be introduced. Jharkhand comprises more than a fourth of the total cultivated area in Bihar, but less than 7 per cent of the irrigation facilities are located in the region. While 30 percent of India's cultivable land is irrigated and the figure for Bihar stands at 27 percent, that of Chhotanagpur is 7 percent only. And significantly, though 80 percent of Biharis annual income is from Chhotanagpur the budgetary expenditure for it is only 10-15 percent.

Jharkhand produces 7 percent of the total electricity generated in India. And per capita consumption of electricity in the Jharkhand is the highest in the country. But the proportion of villages electrified where the vast majority of Jharkandis live, is the lowest in the country as is evident from the table below :

Region	*Per capita Consumption of electricity 1971-72 (KWH)*	*Proportion of villages electrified till March 31, 1973*
Jharkhand	204.4	5.0
Rest of Bihar	19.5	20.1
All India	96.3	27.3

Source : N. Sengupta 'Background of the Jharkhand in *Fourth World Dynamics : Jharkhand*, Authors Guild Publication, New Delhi, 1982, p. 13.

One of the most important foundations of tribal economy is the land. Rev. Cushlaw rightly observes, "The most powerful motive in Santhal life is possession of their lands which they till...the land is the part of the spiritual as well as economic heritage."[11] Referring to Mundas Suresh Singh writes "To them the land was not an arithmetic of a few acres, it was a part of their socio-cultural heritage ; it contained the burial ground of their ancestors with whom they would be united after their death and the sacrificial grave where they propitiated their spirits."[12]

The loss of lands began in the early 17 the century when a large number of Rajputs, Brahmins and Muslims started migrating to the region at the instance of the Mahraja who awarded them grants of lands or villages not as cultivators but as rent collectors.

The situation further deteriorated with the advent of the East India Company. By the beginning of the 19th Century a four-tiered system of administration had developed. At the top was the Company, followed by the Maharaja of Chhotanagpur, then a number of local rajas, mainly, non-tribals and finally intermediary rent-collectors.

It should be mentioned that the tribal protests took the forms of agitations during the British Rule. Mention may be made of the Kole Rebellion in 1832 when the diku thikaders were attacked. Then there were the Santhal revolts during 1885-86. The movement was directed against the Zamindari retainers-gomasthas, peons and Mahajans and their agents—the police, revenue and the court amlas.[13] The Santhal rebellion forced the British to review their tribal policy. An area of 5,000 square miles was carved out as a non-regulation district and administrative machinery was set up for the recovery of alienated lands from immigrant landlords and to return them to the tribal people.

In 1885 there took place the famous Birsa Rebellion which may be regarded as the precursor of the Jharkhand movement. Birsa believed "the ideal order...would witness the liquidation of the recist enemies the Dikas, the European Missionaries and officials and native Christians".[14] It was a movement launched against the prevailing legal and administrative system. The movement pursuaded the British to give a more serious consideration to the land problem. The Chhotanagpur Tenancy Act was passed in 1908 prohibiting further alienation of Munda ancestral lands. But it was too late because by that time most of the lands had already passed into the hands of the immigrant landlords.

Kathleen Gough has regarded the 18th Century movements in the Jharkhand region as "restorative rebellions".[15] The tribals rose in revolt against the British rulers and Hindu zamindars who had encroached upon their lands and against the moneylenders who were extracting surplus from them.

However, land alienation problem assumed alarming proportion in the second half of the 19th Century. The severity of the problem is evident from the outpouring of tribals from the region to the tea plantations in Assam and Bengal. In 1921 nearly a third of the tribal population had emigrated. There were as many as 9.7 lakhs adivasis in Assam tea plantations in 1920-21. Today there are 45 lakh tribals there. The tragedy of migration is etched in their folklore ;

'chol Mini Assam Jabo
Deshe Boro Dukh Re
Assam Deshe Re Mini
Cha Bagan Hariyal'.

(The mother sings to her daughter Mini and says' let us go to Assam for there is only misery here. In Assam there are tea gardens and grenery.) On reaching Assam she sings :

'Sardar Bole Kam Kam
Babu Bole Dhari Aan
Saheb Bole Libc Pither cham
Re Jadu Ram
Phanki Diye Pathali Assam.'[16]

(The supervisor says work, work, catch and bring them back, barks the manager, the Englishman threatens to flay our hide. Jodu Ram—the agent—you have duped us and sent to Assam).

Forest is intimately connected with tribal life and culture. It is the abode of the spirits and the place of worship, the seat of life-cycle ceremonies. It is the source of food and of employment. Forests supplement even the agriculturist tribes by its produce such as firewood, leaves, fruits, honey, grasses etc. "Forest dwelling tribe like Birhor depends on the forest to the extent of 90 per cent, the hill cultivators, Malers get 60 per cent of their livelihood from forest, and agriculturist tribes like Mundas, Oraon and Ho depend on it to the extent of 45 per cent.[17] Evidently, tribal economy rests on forests. Tribal culture is preserved through rites, in myths and by tradition—all linked in some way to the land and forests.

Until about the 19th Century the British forest policy in the tribal belt took care of the tribal interests by allowing them free access to forest products. In 1894 the Government asserted its rights over the forest wealth. The forest officers began to interfere in forest affairs. Gradually, the Government began to stake its complete control over the forest wealth causing a deadly blow to the tribal economy.

After the Independence no significant change has taken place in the field of forest policy. With the gradual extension of settlement and forest codes in those areas many of the administrative problems of the region were for the time being solved, but they brought about a complete transformation of the tribal economic life. After Independence came the Land Reforms Act of 1950 and the Private Protected Forests Act of 1949 which extended uniformly state control over all the tribal regions of Bihar. The state today earns a revenue of Rs. 30 crores from the forests of the Jharkhand region. Tribals are, however, given 'licences' for the collection of certain forest products.

Then, again, many of the forest products such as Kendu leaf, mohua-honey provided secondary means of livelihood to thousands of Jharkhandi families. They collected them from the forests and sold to the traders. Many of these trades have been nationalised.

The forest-based tribal economy has been very hard hit on account of indiscriminate deforestation. The Forest Development Corporation set up in 1975 decided to replace sal trees by teak trees. Sal is a tree every bit of which is used by the tribals, some as food, some as material for building huts etc. Its hard durable timber is used as village carts, beams, the soft kernel of the fruit is eaten by the tribals in lean times and used in choclates. Sal leaves are also shaped into drinking cups in tribal villages. The sal tree is used in tribal religious rites. Both the Mundas and Hos worship certain sal trees described variously as 'Sarna', 'Besale' or 'Zera'.

The missionaries also played a very significant role in organising the tribals and in uniting them for a common cause. The Committee constituted by the Home Ministry in September 1982 under the Chairmanship of B.K. Roy Burman emphasised the importance of forests in tribal life. The Committee noted that after Independence the forestry operations have been regarded as revenue earners for the state and private sector ignoring the needs of the tribals. It was emphasised that the individual tribal, local tribal community and national tribal interest should be the three corners of the future forest policy.

The Government of India had circulated draft resolution on national forest policy. The resolution emphasises that having regard to the symbiotic relationship between the tribal people and the forests all agencies responsible for forest management should associate the tribal people with and development of forests as well as with all attempts to provide gainful employment to the tribals living in and around the forests. The Government of India Committee on Forests and Tribals reported in 1982 that where the tribals were allowed to manage their community forests, they managed the same well.

It is heartening to note that in Chhotanagpur 54,000 acres of *Khunkali* forest was taken over by the state for scientific management in 1947 on promise of paying incremental income to the concerned 'communities.' But while the bureaucratic management led to the depletion of forest thus taken over, no payment has been made to the concerned people. The missionaries played a remarkable role in organising the tribles and uniting them for a common cause. The Christian missionaries arrived in the Chhotanagpur area during 1945 and taught the people the usefulness about the constitutional means for the regaining of their lost lands.[18] It was they who united them under the banner of formal organisations. The Unnati Samaj and Adivasi Mahasabha were constituted at the instance of the missionaries. They supported the cause of tribal people in any struggle against the landlords and moneylenders. As a result the landlord treated them as their enemies. They ran many schools and colleges where the Christian tribals got educated. It was they who took up leadership in many tribal uprisings. Pardeshi says, "Historically the role of Missionaries was that of agents of imperialism but seen in the context of relationship between landlords and poor peasants their role assumes a different menning".[19]

Internal Colonialism Thesis

There is a feeling in some quarters that Jharkhand is a classic case of internal colonialism in India : A.K. Roy has argued that social inequality, regional unevenness in terms of political development and regional economic disparity has created numerous internal colonies in India of which Jharkhand is the biggest and most precious. According to him the first ingredient of internal colonialism is the caste system which has been reinforced by capitalism and turned into racialism. He calls it social unevenness. The second ingredient of internal colonialism is regional unevenness. The tribal areas like Jharkhand in India have become the colonies of the developed area. The third is economic unevenness. The rich and poor here are not only of different classes but of different races socially cut off with a clear distinction. The metropolis of the country has formed nexus with the metropolis of the world. This is what Roy calls true social imperialism enslaving the Indian proletariat. These three ingredients fused together create internal colonialism, among the numerous internal colonies, Jharkhand represents the biggest and most precious internal colony.[20]

The logic of the internal colonialism thesis as discussed above starts from wrong basis. Internal colonialism presupposes an oppressor nationality. The supporters oft he JMM would like to refer to the North Biharis. This would raise the question of the position of the North Bihar in the economic map of India. In fact, Bihar as a whole contributes very little to the total national income of the country. The nature of exploitation to which the poor Jharkhandis are victims, is essentially capitalist. It is wrong to look for "Oasis of such a Jharkhand state within the desert of the Indian Union where exploitation is the rule."[21]

It has been very correctly said that it is dangerous and confusing to compare the position of the Jharkhandis with that in South Africa. It is a mis-statement of fact to suggest that the exploited in the Jharkhand are physically divided in the way they are in South Africa. The Scheduled Caste and Scheduled Tribe population in Jharkhand constitute 47% of the total population in the region. The percentage of exploited must be much higher.

Roy and his associates raise the question of national self determination to support the demand for a separate state. The Marxists should support nationalist movement when they are directed against the feudal oppression or against the colonial oppressor. In India we do not have a single dominant nationality. The big bourgeoisie which rule India with the feudallords as their allies are essentially multinational in character. It is the unity of the toiling masses which can organise struggle for overthrowing the exploitative system. It is the Indian state and capitalist development model India has accepted which generate regional unevenness and facilitate the exploitation of the poor by the rich. If a separate tribal state is set up it will be captured by the tribal elites—the richest section of the tribal population. The poor tribal people will be exploited by the richer section of the tribal population. The Indian capitalist state afriad of the organised strength of the peasantry and working class is trying to break their unity by developing a feeling among the poor tribals that they are being exploited by the non-tribals. It is the bourgeois-landlord state which is the real enemy.

REFERENCES

1. K. Singh, 'Tribal Autonomy Movements in Chhotanagpur' in *Tribal Movements in India*, (ed.), K.S. Singh, Manohar, New Delhi, 1983, p. 5.

2. *Jharkhand State : What, Why, How* ? Church Press, Ranchi, 1979.

3. *Probe India*, March, 1984, p. 45.

4. *Probe India, op. cit.*, p. 56.

5 L.P. Vidyarthi, *Industrialisation in India : A Case Study of Tribal Bihar*, Ranchi University, Ranchi, 1970, p. 59.

6 N. Sengupta, Class and Tribe in Jharkhand, *Economic aud Political Weekly*, 5 April, 1980, p. 667.

7. R. Munda, 'In Search of a Tribal Homeland, *The Statesman*, 4 Feb., 1989.

8. N. Sengupta, *EPW*, *op. cit.*, p. 667.

9. See N. Sengupta, '*The Destitute and the Development : A Study of the Bauri Community in Bokaro Steel City*, Concept Publishers, New Delhi, 1979.

10. A.K. Roy, The Jharkhand Movement and the Question of Internal Colonialism', *Frontier*, Vol. 14, Nos. 35 & 36.

11. Rev. Kushlaw, *The Tribal Heritage : A Study of the Santhals*, quoted by G. Pardeshi in *Mainstream*, 20 July, 1980.

12. S. Singh, *Dust Storm and Hanging Mist : Story of Birsa Munda and His Movement in Chhotanagpur*, K.L. Mukhopadhyay, Calcutta, 1966, p 193.

13. K.K. Dutta, *The Santhal Insurrection, 1855-57*, University of Calcutta, 1940, pp. 7-8.

14. K.S. Singh, *Dust Storm and Hanging Mist : Story of Birso Movement and His Movement in Chhotanagpur*, *op. cit.*, p. 193.

15. K. Gough, *EPW*, Special Number, August, 1974, pp. 1391-92.

16. *Probe India*, *op. cit.*, p. 47.

17. *Mainstream*, August 11, p. 16.

18. See Surjit Sinha, Tribal Solidarity Movements in India in *Tribal Situation in India* : Proceedings of a Seminar, Indian Institute ot Advanced Study, Simla, 1972.

19 G Pardeshi, 'Submerged Masses in Rich Area', *Mainstream*, 20 July, 1980, p. 27.

20. A.K. Roy, *op. cit.*

21. S. Chakraborty, 'Jharkhand Movement and the Working Class' *Frontier*, July, 17, 1982, p. 5.

Index